Dr. Marlin S. Potash

HIDDEN AGENDAS

QUANTITY SALES

Most Dell books are available at special quantity discounts when purchased in bulk by corporations, organizations, and special-interest groups. Custom imprinting or excerpting can also be done to fit special needs. For details write: Dell Publishing, 666 Fifth Avenue, New York, NY 10103. Attn.: Special Sales Department.

INDIVIDUAL SALES

Are there any Dell books you want but cannot find in your local stores? If so, you can order them directly from us. You can get any Dell book in print. Simply include the book's title, author, and ISBN number if you have it, along with a check or money order (no cash can be accepted) for the full retail price plus $2.00 to cover shipping and handling. Mail to: Dell Readers Service, P.O. Box 5057, Des Plaines, IL 60017.

Hidden Agendas

What's REALLY Going On in Your Relationships— in Love, at Work, in Your Family

Dr. Marlin S. Potash

with Susan Meltsner

A Dell Trade Paperback

To Laura
To Hilary
with the strongest wish that your automatic agendas be loving re-
lationships and work you love, your hidden agendas be character-
ized by respect, and your open agendas be filled with acceptance
of yourself and others.
Mama loves you.

AUTHOR'S NOTE

Confidentiality is one of the cornerstones of effective psychotherapy. In order to trust the therapist, the patient must believe that anonymity will be preserved, and the right to privacy must be a given. To that end, all case descriptions in this book, though they stem in great part from my private practice and teaching experience, have been altered so that identifying characteristics and other details have been expunged without loss of flavor of the examples. They are also intended to portray situations in the clearest possible light and, therefore, connections drawn between cause and solution might appear a little more obvious and direct than may occur in real life.

A DELL TRADE PAPERBACK
Published by
Dell Publishing
a division of
Bantam Doubleday Dell Publishing Group, Inc.
666 Fifth Avenue
New York, New York 10103

ISBN: 0-440-50304-3

Reprinted by arrangement with Delacorte Press, New York, New York

Printed in the United States of America

Published simultaneously in Canada

July 1991

10 9 8 7 6 5 4 3 2 1

RRH

Acknowledgments

While any book is more of a collaboration than I ever realized as little as three years ago, I am, of course, responsible for the words and spirit of this one. I have drawn on my experiences treating patients, training therapists, teaching at universities and working in organizations, as well as anything else that might inspire me to stop and pay attention to the agendas we all keep.

Having said that, there are certain people whose help has been invaluable. Professional colleagues and mentors in the fields of psychotherapy, psychiatry and organizational psychology have had an impact on my thinking, often long after the conversations that sparked any response took place. I suppose that is proof positive of the thesis of this book—it certainly holds true in my own life. I want to thank Dr. Harry Levinson for introducing me to his seminal approach to organizational diagnosis. Although the concepts in this book are my own reinterpretations and applications, I remain indebted to him for his brilliant vision and the opportunity to see the world of work relationships from that point of view. Dr. Evan Longin, one of the very finest family therapists I know, continually teaches me about relationships.

My thanks to Emily Marlin, without whom I would never have written this book, and whose prolific work in the field urges me to continue in the face of any momentary doubts. Without the discussion of therapy cases and sharing ideas for how best to assist our patients, the process of psychotherapy would be not only less beneficial to those I treat, but also quite lonely. In this regard, discussions with Dr. Gregg Bergh, the Rev. Maureen Young, Ora Zamir, M.A., Psychology, and Dr. Michael Beldoch sustain me.

I would also like to thank my publishers Leslie Schnur

and Bob Miller; my agent, Bob Markel; and Philip Lief, Cathy Hemming, and Jamie Rothstein, all of whom know just how much their belief in me and this project meant to me along the way. A very special thanks to Susan Meltsner, whose editorial help has been superlative and whose ability to "get" what I have to say and put it into accessible language continues to thrill me.

Andy Garvin shared his own conceptualization of the layers of psyche during many thought-provoking conversations, and Linda Garvin helped me maintain a sense of humor. My husband, Fred Fruitman, has always been there, adding both a business perspective and asking the kinds of questions not always easy to answer, but certainly so crucial for me to address.

As always, my patients and the people in organizations with whom I work have been my most valued resources. Listening to them, and to the feelings and thoughts engendered in me (when I can tolerate them) leads me closer and closer to my own automatic agenda, the most exciting of journeys and one I invite you to take with me, using this book.

Contents

The time which we have at our disposal every day is elastic; the passions that we feel expand it, those that we inspire contract it; and habit fills up what remains.

Marcel Proust
Within a Budding Grove

Introduction

The men and women I treat in my psychotherapy practice, my corporate clients, and the people who ask my advice after hearing me lecture are intelligent, articulate, and hard working. They are also frustrated by situations in their personal and professional lives in which they sense that something is going on below the surface, but cannot figure out exactly what it is or how they can change their circumstances.

"I feel as if I'm receiving vital information in secret code," they say. "I can never be sure that I got the real message."

They look back on conversations and ask themselves: "Did he really mean what he said or was he buttering me up so I would do him a favor?" "Did she just make a pass at me?" "Did I do something to irritate him?" "Am I being paranoid or was there something she wasn't telling me?"

With certain looks, comments, or actions, their relatives, friends, or colleagues often get to them, making them act out of proportion and say things they later regret.

Day in and day out they run into and get bowled over by hidden agendas. They encounter people who conceal, camouflage, or misrepresent their true motives. And they have tried everything they could think of to improve the uncomfortable work situations, bewildering personal relationships, or nerve-wracking family interactions that these hidden agendas create. Yet, all they seem to do is continue running into the same brick wall over and over again. They are at their wit's end, convinced that they have exhausted all their options for dealing with the problem people in their lives. You may feel this way, too, and that may be why this book caught your eye.

If up to this point you have been unable to extract yourself from frustrating or painful circumstances, it is probably not because you have not tried hard enough to solve your problems. There is no doubt in my mind that you have tried —and tried and tried. The trouble lies not with the amount of effort you put into coping with manipulative people and baffling situations, but with where you have directed your energy and how you have viewed your circumstances. You have been repeatedly looking at them through the same lens and automatically trying the only solutions that seem viable from that limited angle. What I offer my patients and what I offer you in this book is a new vantage point from which you can recognize the wide array of options you actually have, and choose the ones that will work for you.

Like the men and women who walk into my office, sit across from me in corporate conference rooms, or corner me in lecture halls, you may be looking for a way to psyche out other people, to read their hidden agendas and figure out how to keep them from getting to you. You want them to stop pushing your buttons and making your life miserable. I have written this book to help you do that—in what I believe is the only truly effective way to do so—by figuring out where your buttons really are and why you react the way you do to those problem people in your life.

By the time you reach the final pages of this book, you will know how and why people knowingly or unwittingly keep secrets from you. You will also know why you find yourself in messes that bear an uncanny resemblance to messes you have been in before—as if you were destined to suffer the same disappointments, get involved with the same types of "impossible" people, or even have the same arguments over and over again. You will recognize your own habitual responses to events or relationships that do not proceed as you expected—knee-jerk reactions like becoming sullen, sarcastic, or vindictive.

You will be able to stop telling yourself angrily that you would "not be in this mess" if you were not so stupid, to stop blaming yourself for circumstances beyond your control or feeling helpless in the face of things you can change, and stop trying to make the world behave the way you think it should. Equally important, you will finally realize that you, too, conceal, camouflage, or misrepresent *your* true thoughts, feelings, motives, or intentions. In other words, that you have a few hidden agendas of your own.

As you get a handle on all the secret-keeping that goes on between you and others in your work setting, your family, or your circle of friends, you can begin to solve the puzzles of everyday living.

Let me give you an in-depth example of hidden agendas in action:

David, the head of one product division of an import company, had created the job of development director just for Bart. Bart's office was supposed to serve as a clearinghouse for the entire division, the place where everything came together and was coordinated.

However, when any of the staff consulted with Bart, they quickly discovered that he never knew the answers to their questions, so they took them to someone who did—Stephanie, the marketing coordinator, who had unofficially run the department prior to Bart's arrival, and who shortly afterward became a patient of mine.

"Bart is in charge," David had asserted. "What he says goes." But Bart for the most part said nothing, or changed his mind a dozen times during any given day, or made inappropriate requests, such as asking secretaries to type his personal correspondence. In no time flat he infuriated his entire staff, and they brought their complaints to Stephanie, who listened patiently, calmed them down, and usually found a temporary solution to their problems. Even the division's customers and other department heads circumvented Bart and consulted Stephanie. They knew they could count on her to get the job done—and had tired of waiting for Bart to return their calls.

In short, even though Bart had been given the official title, the authority that came with it, and twice the salary she earned, Stephanie was still running the department—and continued to do so for more than a year.

Does that seem unlikely—or all too familiar? An indispensable underling holds things together for a scatterbrained manager who "gets away with murder" is a minidrama played out in many business settings. It always raises a few questions. First, how did Bart—who had neither the know-how nor the work habits to run a department—get the job in the first place and why didn't he lose it after his incompetence became obvious to everyone around him?

Second, why did Stephanie—who was not being paid or officially recognized for running the department—do Bart's job for him and continue to do it long after working twelve to fourteen hour days began to take a physical and emotional toll on her?

Third, was David—who acted as if nothing was amiss—truly unaware of the situation? Or did he know about it but chose not to deal with it? Why would he make such a choice?

And last, how did the entire staff and everyone who dealt with the division manage to come to the exact same conclusion—that it was better to put up with and work around Bart than to mention their problems to David or someone else with the power to correct them?

Based on the information available to them, the staff and clientele of the import company could not answer those questions. Indeed, their circumstances made no more sense to them than they do to us as outside observers. What's more, everyone involved knew that somewhere down the line their house of cards would collapse. It seemed inevitable that Bart would make a mistake that could not be ignored or that Stephanie would get fed up and quit. Yet in spite of the sense of impending doom that hung over them, they all continued to play their parts as written, never deviating from the script or questioning the direction in which the play was going. You will learn later in the book how this minidrama was resolved. And you will also learn how to resolve any in which you are now playing a starring or supporting role.

When you encounter hidden agendas and the baffling situations they create, you have three options: you can *change yourself*—your attitudes, expectations, or habits, the way you feel about yourself and about other people's behavior, or your responses to their behavior. You can *change your circumstances*—your job, the amount of time you spend with people who irritate you versus the people whose company you enjoy, the activities you involve yourself in, so you will expand your circle of friends, and so on. Or you can *drive yourself crazy.* This book will show you how to make use of the first two options so you do not have to get stuck with the third. But more importantly, you will have gained new insights and awareness that will enable you to make choices that are in your best interest, and break self-defeating behavior patterns in your professional and personal life. In short, this book has the potential to take you wherever you want to go, but it may not get you there in quite the way you expected.

What Can You Expect
from This Book?

Throughout my career as a psychotherapist and organizational consultant, men and women from all walks of life have come to me for answers—the same answers you may be hoping to find between the covers of this book. When they arrive at my office or corner me after a speech, they invariably expect me to give them those answers, to tell them what is really going on in their lives or relationships and exactly what they should do. They believe that I can solve the mysteries of everyday living for them—and you may too. So let me set the record straight and reveal my agenda by telling you what I tell them.

Would that I were so wise as to have all the answers. I do not. Nor am I presumptuous enough to tell you what you should do with your life. In fact, you would be foolish to listen to me if I did. If I lucked out and actually solved your immediate problem, the next time you encountered a baffling situation, bewildering relationship, or mysterious interaction, you would be no better off than you were before. And believe me, for the duration of your stay on this planet, you will continue to encounter curve balls and trick pitches. That does not mean that you should duck for cover or get out of the game entirely. It would be in your best interest, however, to become a better batter, and that is something I can help you to do.

As a psychotherapist, my job is to help my patients look at things differently so they can have a wider array of choices than they have had in the past. That is also the goal of this book. Rather than solving mysteries for you, it will show you where to look for clues and encourage you to piece them together in the way that fits your personality, needs, and circumstances.

Although the term "hidden agendas" may conjure up images of willful deception and malicious people who intentionally conceal their true motives in order to manipulate or hurt you, I use the phrase in a much broader, deeper manner. This book is based on the premise that all of us are "wired" from childhood to act and react in certain ways and that we are not always conscious of why we do what we do or even what we are doing while we are doing it.

For instance, when you go through your daily routines, perform certain aspects of your job, address your boss in one tone of voice and your children in another, look for oncoming cars before crossing the street, or otherwise conduct yourself comfortably and appropriately in many diverse settings, you do so without much or any conscious thought or in-depth analysis over the alternatives available to you. You operate on *auto-pilot.*

Operating on auto-pilot is not about what you say or do, but rather how and why you say or do things. For example, suppose that you get home from work feeling tired and frazzled, go to the freezer, take out the chocolate ice cream, scoop some into a dish and eat it. If you are fully aware of feeling tired and frazzled, realize that eating ice cream is something you sometimes do to comfort yourself when you feel that way, consider what else you could do to meet your needs, and then choose to eat the ice cream, you are making a conscious decision and are *not* on auto-pilot. On the other hand, if every day after work you immediately head for the freezer, numbly swallowing spoonful after spoonful of ice cream, then you are on auto-pilot, being driven by instinct, habit, or needs that are outside your awareness.

As I tell my patients, operating on auto-pilot provides a useful shortcut for dealing with many of the details of daily living, especially routine interactions in which little is at stake. However, situations and relationships rife with hidden agendas do *not* fall into that category. Bypassing logic and reason in baffling situations is rarely in our best interest, yet most of us do just that. We keep secrets because that is the familiar, comfortable thing for us to do and not necessarily because the immediate circumstances actually warrant it. We react to other people's hidden agendas automatically, using the same responses we have used since childhood—even though they do not necessarily fit that particular situation or may have stopped working for us in general.

This book can help you operate on a more conscious, insightful level, giving you more control and access to more options. To do that you need to understand what makes people tick, and the first person you must come to understand is yourself.

Toward that end, this book takes you on an archaeological expedition. First it reveals what you have hidden just below the surface, the secrets that you knowingly keep, and what you hope to accomplish by doing so. Then it digs deeper, uncovering the needs, fears, wishes, and expectations that may be as much a mystery to you as they are to others, because they reside in your *psychological blind spots.*

When you were learning to drive, you heard about blind spots—the areas that remain outside your line of vision while you are driving your car. Well, that phenomenon provides an excellent metaphor for the places *within yourself* that you cannot see. We all have these psychological blind spots; and contrary to what you might be imagining, they are most often *not* dark, bottomless pits, black holes in your psyche with countless demons lurking in the shadows. They generally conceal two or three pivotal secrets at most—two or three issues that you repeatedly sideswipe or have headlong collisions with. They are apt to be issues like dealing with intimacy, authority, control, aggression, sexuality, guilt or conflict, as well as behavior patterns such as:

- the martyr complex (constantly trying to save people who are unsavable or taking on herculean tasks that are not actually your responsibility);
- the "I'll be happy when . . ." syndrome (believing that you will finally be able to enjoy life when you make enough money, lose fifty pounds, or your kids grow up. Unfortunately, while you are waiting for these momentous events to occur, the life you could be living is now passing you by);
- the "shoulda, woulda, coulda" routine (spinning your wheels and going nowhere by rehashing the past and blaming yourself—or others—rather than taking mistakes into account while living in an imperfect world).

Your blind spots contain information that you could factor into the decisions you make, increasing the likelihood that those decisions would be in your best interest. They prevent you from seeing the potholes in the road ahead of you or the eighteen-wheeler about to overtake you and run you off the highway. Thus, in spite of our natural fear of exploring uncharted territory, bringing to light some of what you have hidden in your blind spot is not nearly as dangerous as continuing to blithely roll along as if that material did not exist or influence you at all.

None of us ever gets rid of our blind spots completely. However, *Hidden Agendas* can help you become more aware of where your blind spots are, what forces they are hiding from view, and how these forces influence your thoughts, feelings, and behavior. It can help you gain insight (the psychological equivalent of your car's rear-view and side-view mirrors) into the unsettling information you filed away and forgot about, but which reappears in the characteristic responses you rely on whenever external circumstances threaten you in any way. But insight without change is of intellectual curiosity only—not very useful. Even if you cannot entirely rid yourself of blind spots, you can compensate for them, better protecting yourself (and your passengers), becoming more proficient in other areas of your life.

As you come to understand yourself and what makes you tick, you also learn a great deal about other people and what makes them tick. This book may begin primarily with you, but it will also help you understand other people's motives and methods, the interplay and connections between their agendas and yours, the unspoken, presumed-to-be-agreed-upon rules for your relationships and what happens when someone knowingly or unwittingly breaks the rules.

The third and final section of this book shows you how to get off auto-pilot, reduce the emotional charge of baffling interactions, increase your options and consciously, insightfully decide what to do in difficult situations. It helps you change what you can change—yourself (how you interpret and respond to baffling situations) or your circumstances. It enables you to stop driving yourself crazy by operating on auto-pilot and hating yourself afterward, or trying to change what you cannot change, most notably other people.

Overall, you can think of this book as being much like the operator's manuals that come with your personal computer or automobile. The computer manual does not dictate what you use your computer for and the automobile manual does not tell you where to drive your car. Likewise, this book does not tell you how to live your life. Instead, it explains how the equipment (your psyche) works and suggests ways to keep yourself in peak operating condition. That way, no matter what you encounter in your life, you still have options and are able to make conscious choices that are in your best interest.

Now that my agenda—to help you gain insight and resources for coping with hidden agendas and the baffling situations they create—is out in the open, let's begin by taking a look at some of those baffling situations and the conclusions most of us jump to whenever we encounter them. As you will see, what you don't know *can*—and often does—hurt you.

1

Dreadfully Puzzled?

Why What You Don't Know *Can* Hurt You

"Alice felt dreadfully puzzled. The Hatter's remark seemed to her to have no meaning in it, and yet it was certainly English."

Lewis Carroll
Alice's Adventures in Wonderland

Without tumbling down a rabbit hole or traveling through a looking glass, we all encounter people as puzzling as the Mad Hatter, and feel every bit as bewildered as Alice did in Wonderland. At any given moment, in boardrooms and bedrooms, at business lunches and on blind dates, the behavior we observe and the words we hear may not tell the whole story—or worse yet, may make little or no sense to us at all.

Whether we encounter these mysteries of everyday living at work, in our intimate relationships, with family members, or within the confines of our own minds, what we don't know *can* hurt us—leaving us baffled at best and more often than not anxious and insecure, frustrated and furious, or helpless and downright depressed.

What's Going On?

——

At Work

Barry paced. Back and forth, back and forth across his office he retraced an eight-step path while his thoughts circled round an eight-word question—"What am I going to do about Eddie?"

Eddie, a counselor at a substance-abuse treatment center, had been a thorn in Barry's side from the start. Barry, recently hired to supervise counselors, could not think of a single encounter with Eddie that proceeded smoothly, and considering what had just happened he was beginning to wonder if one ever would.

After the weekly staff meeting which Eddie—for the second week in a row—failed to attend, Barry summoned him to his office. *"Maybe this time I'll get through to him,"* Barry said to himself. But he never got the chance. Eddie interrupted Barry's carefully worded reprimand almost immediately.

"I'm the senior counselor on the detox unit," he said, "and if you want me at your stupid meetings, you should pick up the phone and call me."

Eddie's comment was so unexpected and made so little sense to Barry that he was rendered speechless.

What is he talking about? Barry asked himself. *He couldn't possibly expect a personal invitation to each and every staff meeting.*

But what does *he want and why is he always giving me such a hard time?* When Eddie left the office, Barry paced and pondered the question that I so often hear from both labor and management—*What's really going on here?*

Whether you work in a hospital, a factory, a restaurant, a department store, or for a Fortune 500 company; whether you are the chief executive officer, a computer programmer, a construction foreman, a sales clerk, or a social worker, your interactions at work—like Barry's confrontation with Eddie—can leave you awash in a sea of confusion. In addition to insubordinate subordinates such as Eddie, the work world is full of little, seemingly unsolvable mysteries—as you well know if you:

- work for a boss who doesn't specify what he wants but jumps all over you for not doing it;
- supervise an employee who seemed bright and eager during her interview but who still has not learned the proper procedures after six months on the job, no matter how many times you explain them;
- contend with a superior who constantly urges you to show initiative, but shoots down every idea you propose, or worse yet, presents your idea as if it were his own;
- feel tense in the presence of a boss, coworker, or client who slips sexual innuendos into every conversation;
- are expected to "work around" an incompetent employee because no one is willing to face the problem or try to correct it.

Of course, the workplace is not the only setting in which such bewildering situations are found. The men and women I treat in my psychotherapy practice offer living proof that marriages and other intimate relationships provide fertile ground for interactions that leave us scratching our heads and wondering what's really going on.

In Intimate Relationships

Michael, a thirty-two-year-old graphic artist, recently came home from work to find his wife, Kate, a twenty-eight-year-old magazine editor, seated at the kitchen table reading through a stack of manuscripts that she had brought home from the office. When she pulled away as he tried to kiss her and appeared disinterested in his attempts to make conversation, Michael assumed that Kate had to get her work done and wanted to be left alone. He took a beer from the refrigerator and went into the living room to watch the end of the 6 o'clock news.

A few moments after settling down on the sofa, Michael heard Kate banging things around in the kitchen, and making other sounds of discontent. "Uh-oh. What did I do now?" he thought and got up to find out.

"Is something bothering you?" Michael asked.

"What could possibly be bothering me?" Kate replied.

"I don't know. That's why I'm asking you to tell me," he said calmly, although he was entertaining fantasies of wringing her neck.

"There's nothing to tell," Kate insisted, turning her back to him and pounding a veal cutlet in much the way he assumed she wanted to pound his head. Well aware that there was indeed something to tell, but knowing from past experience that Kate would not tell until she was good and ready, Michael shrugged and returned to the living room.

They ate dinner in tense silence, despite Michael's inquiries about Kate's day and his attempts at humor. Afterward, Kate took her work and holed up in their bedroom. When Michael came to bed several hours later, Kate pretended to be asleep.

According to Michael, who described the entire incident to me at the couple's next therapy session, he called Kate from his office the next day. "The first thing she said was 'Oh, so today you have time for me,' " he reported. "And that's when I figured out what was going on."

It seems that the day before, Kate had called just as Michael was on his way out to a meeting. "So I told her that I was busy and couldn't talk," Michael continued. "I couldn't help thinking, 'She gave me the silent treatment for *that?*' Did she think that I didn't *want* to talk to her, that I was lying or what? I mean, what was the big deal? I just don't get it."

Like Michael, many of us just don't "get" what goes on between ourselves and our spouses or lovers. Even though we are intimately involved with these people and have close, long-standing relationships with them, they do not always think, feel or act as we expect them to. Indeed, they sometimes seem like creatures from another planet, who interpret the world around them much differently than we do. "If I live to be 110, I'll never understand this person," my patients say. "I'll never know how this person will react or what I'm supposed to do to make our relationship work."

You, too, may be hit by a wave of insecurity, anger, or confusion as you struggle to figure out *why:*

- your spouse seems less interested in having sex than he or she formally did;
- your wife is suddenly feeling pressured about going back to school or getting a job;
- you panic each time the man or woman you love seems to be hinting around about marriage or living together;
- the man or woman you love panics each time you hint around about marriage or living together;
- your lover, who is obviously under a great deal of stress at work, brushes you off each time you try to get him to talk about his feelings;
- your former boyfriend—who broke up with *you*—

keeps calling to ask what you want him to do with the stuff you left in his apartment, even though you have already answered that question at least a dozen times; your ex-wife never has the kids ready for their weekend visits, invites you to come in for a cup of coffee while you wait for them, and then starts some kind of argument.

While the baffling situations you experience in your intimate relationships or marriages may be the most painful, your memories of—and ongoing involvement with—members of the family you grew up in are apt to be the most infuriating. Indeed, because they have in one way or another puzzled or overwhelmed you in the past, almost anything they do in the present can leave you wondering why they are "doing it to you" again.

Between Family Members

On the fourth day of Jane's most recent visit to her thirty-year-old daughter, Sara, the two women appeared to be having an amiable conversation while Sara prepared dinner. However, an astute observer might have noticed the tension in the air, especially when Sara put a casserole into the oven and Jane, casually moving closer to the stove, glanced at the temperature dial.

"Don't you have this set too high?" she asked.

"No, Mother," Sara replied. "I've made that casserole dozens of times and I always use that setting."

"Well, I guess you know what you're doing," Jane said in a noticeably skeptical tone of voice.

In a flash, Sara reeled around. Her hands placed squarely on her hips and her eyes flashing fire, she shouted, "Believe it or not, Mother, I know how to cook. I know how to clean.

I know how to take care of my husband and my daughter. So why don't you just stop looking over my shoulder and giving me advice that I didn't ask for and I don't need!"

Why is she yelling at me? Jane asked herself. *I was only trying to help.*

I shouldn't have yelled like that, Sara thought, *but for God's sake, when is she going to stop trying to run my life?*

Having in all likelihood experienced some variation of this classic parent/adult-child interaction yourself, you know all too well that no matter how old you are or how drastically your life changes, your parents, children, sisters, and brothers —even when well intentioned—seem to have a never-ending capacity to induce crippling guilt, blind rage, and a maelstrom of other unsettling emotions. In addition to Jane and Sara, perhaps you can identify with:

- the sixty-two-year-old widower whose daughter encourages him to date, but vociferously objects to every "woman friend" he brings around;
- the forty-five-year-old salesman whose younger brother has not visited their invalid mother in over a year, but nonetheless has plenty to say about the quality of care she receives in a nursing home his older brother picked out;
- the countless men and women who just can't understand why their entire families pretend that Grandma does not have Alzheimer's, that their little brother is not experimenting with drugs, or that the bruises on their big sister's body couldn't possibly have been caused by her brutish husband.

In Your Own Mind

Finally, and as if other people's behavior wasn't troublesome enough, we often confuse ourselves. We think, feel, and act in ways that we cannot readily explain, doing and saying things that were never part of any conscious plan. Ever wonder what's really going on in your own head?

Jenny does. This former elementary school teacher recently made a career change and now works for a computer company, training teachers how to use the company's computer software in their classrooms. At forty-two, she was thrilled with her new job and confident that she would do it well since she knew a great deal about both her audience and her product. Unfortunately, her first in-school presentation was, as she put it, "a real shocker."

As she began to speak, Jenny felt relaxed and well-prepared. But several minutes later, she noticed a man in the third row who looked bored. She suspected that he knew more about computers than she did. "I don't know what made me think that," she shrugged. "But I began throwing in more technical details just in case it was true."

Every few seconds she glanced at the man she had labeled a "chip head" and could not help noticing that her informed delivery was not winning him over. In the meantime, several other people began fidgeting in their seats. Hoping to recapture their attention, Jenny told a convoluted anecdote about her own classroom experiences. Then someone asked a question. Her attempt to answer it sent her off on another tangent. And so it went, until she and her audience were so confused that she could think of no alternative but to start the morning coffee break twenty minutes ahead of schedule—ten minutes before the coffee and Danish were brought up from the cafeteria.

What's happening to me? she wondered while frantically

rearranging her note cards. *I know this material like the back of my hand. Why do I keep getting off the track?*

Like Jenny, your best-laid plans and good intentions sometimes are sabotaged by your own bewildering behavior —behavior that seems beyond your control at the moment it occurs and, in retrospect, completely off the wall. You shake your head in utter disbelief and ask yourself why on earth you:

- told a very personal story to a brand-new acquaintance;
- agreed to do something that you did *not* want to do;
- snapped at your spouse, children, parents, or coworkers and immediately felt overwhelmed with guilt;
- left something undone at work, stayed up half the night worrying about it and went in to work at five in the morning to complete the task—which no one would ever have known had it been done the day before;
- felt attracted to someone until he or she showed interest in return, then immediately spotted a "fatal flaw" that eliminated him or her as a potential partner?

Whether they occur at work, in your intimate relationships, with members of your family, or in the confines of your own mind, the circumstances I have just described and countless situations like them have several elements in common. First of all, *something below the surface is motivating our own or someone else's behavior.* Why did Eddie constantly give Barry a hard time? Why did Kate—without any evidence to support her conclusion—react as if Michael had intentionally snubbed her when she called? Why did Sara "flip out" over a comment from her mother that was just irritating at most? And why did Jenny—who did in fact know her material—get so far off track? If they know the answers (and they may not), they are not revealing them to the other person in the interaction and the hidden motives and other secret elements of the situation are what make it so frustrating.

Second, *you can sense that more is going on than meets the eye.* Sometimes you "smell a rat" during the interaction—as Michael did when he heard Kate stomping around in the kitchen and thought, *Uh-oh. What did I do now?* Similarly, while your boss or spouse is speaking to you, you may be wondering, What is he really trying to tell me? While someone usually stingy with praise makes flattering remarks, you may be asking yourself, Is she actually complimenting me or just buttering me up so I'll do her a favor?

In other instances, the oddities hit you after the fact. Only as you are walking away from an interaction or thinking about it hours or even days later, does it strike you that there was something fishy about it. *That did not go at all the way I expected it to,* you think. *I didn't do anything to deserve that sort of treatment,* you decide. *She was lying to me,* you conclude. *Was he coming on to me?* you wonder. *I know this material like the back of my hand, so why do I keep getting off the track?* Jenny thought *after* her presentation had gone far afield.

Or over an extended period of time, your gut instincts may tell you that something is out of whack in an ongoing relationship or on a day-to-day basis. Little signs that all is not well at home or at work accumulate, leaving you generally dissatisfied, vaguely confused, repeatedly frustrated, or constantly bickering and complaining. Like Barry, who agonized over his many run-ins with Eddie and asked himself, *What does he want from me and why is he always blowing up that way?*, you wonder why your spouse keeps picking fights right before bedtime, or when your boss will realize that you can get the job done without him constantly looking over your shoulder. Regardless of when you become aware of it, an interaction or relationship takes on the trappings of a mystery novel as soon as you notice that surface cues (the actions you can see and the words you hear) do not tell the whole story.

Unfortunately, we are not mind readers or even particularly good guessers when it comes to figuring out other people's underlying motives, thoughts, or feelings. Indeed, when vital details are missing from the picture and the messages you are receiving seem to be in some secret code, you may be completely unprepared to crack the code and figure out what is really going on. You may even resent the fact that you are being put in a position to do so.

"For Pete's sake," Michael protested after Kate insisted he should have known that his abrupt disconnection of her call would upset her. "If I tried to figure out what might be on your mind or anyone else's before every little move I make, I'd spend so much time calculating that I wouldn't be able to *do* anything!"

Michael's point is well taken. Attempting, at all times and in all situations, to discern our own and everyone else's underlying motives and probable reactions would leave us paralyzed, and a bit paranoid to boot. However, the fact of the matter is that most of us go to the opposite extreme. While immersed in the rational pursuits of daily living, our frame of reference is often limited to what we are actually doing at a given moment or plan to do in the near future. Operating on auto-pilot, we pay almost no attention to *why* we are doing what we are doing, how our actions affect other people or theirs affect us. Consequently, when something unexpected or unpleasant happens, we may be at a complete loss to explain it. All too often and based on ambiguous signals, we jump to premature conclusions that can turn baffling situations into disastrous ones.

What Happens Next?
—

RECALL EXERCISE 1

Think back to a baffling situation that you recently encountered, the last time you worried about what was really going
on, or a relationship that confused or frustrated you.

> What was happening on the surface? (What was actually
> said or done?)
>
> What made you think that something was also going on
> below the surface?
>
> In reference to those circumstances, how might you have
> completed a sentence that began "I wish I knew . . ."
>
> How did you feel during the interaction?
>
> What thoughts ran through your mind?
>
> What did you decide was going on?
>
> Based on that decision, what did you do? How do you
> feel now about the conclusion you drew then and
> what you did based on it?

When I ask my patients to complete this self-awareness
exercise, their responses almost always point out the final element that various mysteries of everyday living have in common—you rarely feel satisfied with the outcome of such an
interaction or confident that you handled the situation effectively. In fact, as you may have discovered yourself, your
guesses about what was really going on and the course of
action you pursued based on those guesses did not extract
you from the sticky situation at all. Indeed, you may have dug
yourself in deeper, especially if you jumped to one of the five
conclusions I am about to describe.

Conclusion One:

This is a dangerous situation. If I don't figure out what's really going on, something terrible is going to happen.

Consequence: Anxiety

"Whenever Eddie's around, I feel like I'm walking through a mine field," Barry complained to me one day. "I never know what's going to set off that hair trigger of his. I'm always thinking 'If I say this or do that, will he explode or won't he?' And I just never know."

Eddie's unpredictable behavior activated an early warning system in Barry's psyche. Each time he came face-to-face with Eddie (or expected to), signals of impending danger flashed through his mind and he went on "red alert" status, worrying, watching, and anticipating the worst. The baffling situations and bewildering people in your life are apt to have a similar effect on you, convincing you that *no matter what happens, you are not going to like it.*

If I don't get a handle on this right this very instant, you think, I'm going to say or do the wrong thing. I'm going to look foolish, or do or say something I'll later regret. The consequence of having thoughts like these rumbling through your mind like a runaway train is anxiety—which can be most succinctly described as a vague, very unpleasant feeling of fear and apprehension.

In certain situations and manageable doses, anxiety is inevitable and can, in fact, be beneficial. Keeping you alert, it can enable you to foresee problems that you can prepare to handle. However, hypervigilance or too high a level of anxiety interferes with your ability to function or even to think effectively—which was precisely the toll the explosive encounters with Eddie took on Barry.

"I've got myself so worked up about the problems with Eddie that I can barely concentrate on anything else," Barry continued. "When I know I'm going to have to deal with him, my heart starts racing. My hands shake. I get dizzy and I feel like I can't breathe. I know that sounds nuts and I try not to let him see it, but he really has me on edge, and I end up snapping at other counselors who certainly don't deserve to be snapped at."

Other unnerving symptoms of anxiety include waves of feelings that well up at inopportune moments—continually replaying every detail, intrusive or distracting thoughts, and general jumpiness. Any or all can be the by-product of a baffling situation.

Conclusion Two:

I can't cope with this situation. Since I don't have all of the facts, I can't figure out what I'm supposed to do.

Consequence: Stress

When I met Jenny, six months had passed since her first in-school presentation. Each subsequent attempt to do her job had netted similarly disastrous results, and she was in danger of being fired. But that was not why she came to me for therapy. "The job is a problem," she said. "But it's not *the* problem. What I need help with is being tired all the time and wishy-washy. I can't seem to make even the simplest decisions without waffling back and forth a million times. I've been getting headaches, too, and even though I'm exhausted,

I can't seem to relax. Sometimes I think I must be having a nervous breakdown." Actually, what Jenny was experiencing was a physical and emotional reaction to excess stress. And the stress overload she was suffering from was a side effect of the bewildering events that occurred each time she tried to do her job.

"Things never go the way I expect them to," Jenny said. "People don't react the way I want them to. They ask questions I'm not ready to hear and I'm not sure I can answer. After each presentation, I try to account for those things, to plan for them. But then something else goes wrong. I dread going to work because I know that *I won't be able to handle* what happens."

Whenever you are called upon to "handle what happens"—to respond to demands, constraints or even to positive opportunities—you experience stress. Since responses of some kind are required of you constantly throughout each day, you are never completely free of stress and should not expect to be. However, excess stress or stress overload can be debilitating, and you experience it whenever the demands you face actually exceed your ability to handle them, and even more so if you, like Jenny, decide in advance that you are incapable of handling those demands. Unfortunately, you cannot help but decide that when faced with situations in which you sense that something is going on below the surface, but cannot determine what it is.

You see, because you cannot decode your own or other people's baffling behavior, your *coping skills*—what you would normally do to deal with certain circumstances or while interacting with certain people—are incapacitated. More important, and more harmful in the long run, the frustration, anger, or confusion you feel causes you to lose both your objectivity and your faith in your *coping resources*—the backup reservoir of skills you would draw from if you thought they would work. Lacking both the information and the confidence you need to make decisions and solve problems effectively, you are stymied each time you try to figure out how to handle the situations you are facing. The gap between the demands of daily living and your perceived ability to deal with those demands widens and your stress level skyrockets, saddling you with problems like those Jenny experienced as well as a wide range of other unpleasant consequences, such as exhaustion, emotional depletion, insomnia, and feeling all keyed up. A whole rash of other nonspecific physical responses might range from head to stomach to back ailments.

Conclusion Three:

I'll never get to the bottom of this or figure out the right way to handle things. This situation is hopeless and I might as well give up.

Consequence: Depression

You are most likely to draw this self-defeating conclusion if you have repeatedly failed to solve or cope with a recurring mystery in your life. You take the anger, indignation, fear, and frustration generated by situations in which hidden motives are operating, and bottle those emotions up, pushing them down deep inside of you, numbing all of your other feelings as well and going through the motions of daily living like a zombie. Or you aim your anger at yourself, blaming yourself for the pain and frustration you experience, beating yourself up with reminders of what you could have and should have done and ultimately convincing yourself that you are an inadequate, unlovable, helpless, and hopeless human being.

Thus, frustration gives way to depression. Convinced that you are completely helpless to do anything about the bewildering circumstances you have encountered, you close up shop and stop trying to understand or solve the problems in your life or relationships. *If this situation is going to improve,* you think, *either something "out there" must change* (without any effort on your part) *or someone must miraculously come along to rescue me.* Since neither of these wishes is likely to be fulfilled, you get stuck with your unsolved mysteries and unsatisfying relationships. And you get depressed.

"I don't know why I keep planning seven-day trips to my daughter's," Jane said. "By the fourth or fifth day, I can barely drag myself out of bed in the morning. I lie there fighting back tears, wondering where I went wrong while I was raising Sara, what I did to make her hate me so much. My husband and my other kids tell me that she doesn't hate me. But if she doesn't, why is she always so annoyed with me? No matter what I say, she yells or gets huffy. Sometimes I'll come home from a visit and spend a whole day in bed, just looking at the pictures I took while I was at Sara's and crying my eyes out."

Conclusion Four:

Something is going on here, but I don't know what it is. Therefore, I'd better watch my back, cover my ass, get the other person before I'm attacked, and make sure not to make a move until somebody else does.

Consequence: Job Dissatisfaction

This defensive posture, which is an extremely common reaction to hidden agendas in the workplace, may be adopted in response to a supervisor's manipulative management style; the presence of an abrasive, malingering, or grandstanding coworker; the demand to satisfy customers who repeatedly alter or never reveal their expectations; or to changes and unpredictable conditions in the organization itself.

For instance, the fact that Bart was getting away with murder while Stephanie was running herself ragged managing his department did not go unnoticed by anyone directly involved with the products division of the import company I described in the introduction.

Complaints and comments were made in elevators and washrooms, around water coolers, and occasionally to Stephanie. However, no one ever said anything directly to Bart or took their concerns to David or anyone else who could actually do something about the situation. It was as if they all had signed in blood a solemn oath *not* to openly acknowledge certain facts or feelings to certain people and *not* to rock the boat by attempting to remedy the problem—even though it was adversely affecting them.

In addition to this sort of collusion (an unspoken agreement to avoid confronting unpleasant issues or inevitable changes), baffling situations in the workplace make a significant contribution to low morale and low productivity, not to mention absenteeism, accidents, and even wildcat walkouts. What's more, the fact that many people with different personalities and points of view interact with each other countless times each day, and that these people may define their work roles differently (as well as have conflicting ideas about how to exercise and respond to authority), frequently causes tension, misperceptions, and work-related stress. This not only leads to insecurity and dissatisfaction on the job, but can also bleed through into all corners of our lives.

Conclusion Five:

If he is hiding his true thoughts, feelings, and motives from me, then I must hide mine from him. That way we will avoid a fight and our relationship will not be damaged or destroyed.

Consequence: Unsatisfying Relationships

This is the conclusion we are apt to draw whenever we are involved in any kind of ongoing relationship with someone who seems to be keeping something from us or when we ourselves want to avoid conflict. As you probably can tell, it is a response that makes it difficult if not impossible for two people to live happily ever after. Here is an example:

As their romantic getaway weekend drew to a close, twenty-six-year old Carol and her boyfriend Jeff, thirty-two, sat on a sand dune watching the ocean waves lap at the shore and the sky put on its sunset light show.

"When I'm back at work tomorrow, I'm really going to miss this place." Carol sighed, and then, slipping her arm through Jeff's and placing her head on his shoulder, whispered tenderly, "I'm going to miss you too."

Jeff's instantaneous response to this comment was unexpected, to say the least. "Did I ever tell you about the weekend Felicia and I spent here?" he asked, and without waiting for Carol's reply, proceeded to tell a story she would not have wanted to hear under any circumstances and which, under the immediate circumstances, made her feel as if Jeff had slapped her in the face. *Why are you doing this,* she wondered as hurt and angry feelings churned inside her. *Why are you ruining a tender moment by talking about some old girlfriend?*

Now, Carol might have posed those questions or expressed her feelings directly to Jeff, but because she concluded that doing so might precipitate an argument or sever what she feared was a very slender thread holding their relationship together, she did not. Instead, she announced that they needed to go back to the beach house and pack. On the drive home, she "remembered" that she had scheduled an early meeting for the next day and decided not to spend the night at Jeff's place. And for the next few weeks, she placed few calls to Jeff and did not always return his calls immediately. She made plans that did not include him and gave excuses not to see him; not to signal that something was wrong, the way Kate did to Michael, but to put some distance between herself and Jeff—which she had guessed was what Jeff wanted.

In this instance, Carol had guessed right. Distance *was* what Jeff wanted—to a point. But Carol eventually moved beyond that point and Jeff began to feel miserable too. With flowers, cards, inquiries about the state of their relationship made through mutual friends and so on, Jeff sent out signals that he cared and wanted to be close to Carol again. Jeff reeled Carol back in and they both felt comfortable in the relationship—until the next time Carol showed signs of wanting to get closer, whereby Jeff responded by bringing up an untimely topic and the entire cycle began again.

As a result of their attempts to preserve their relationship while concealing their true thoughts, feelings, and motives, the relationship began to resemble a yo-yo. With the exception of the brief periods they spent feeling as close as they both secretly wanted to be, either Carol or Jeff, or both, were miserable.

Concluding that the mysterious elements of your relationship are harbingers of doom, and countering someone's baffling behavior with a few secretly motivated maneuvers of your own lead to numerous repercussions, including:

- adding an emotional charge to minor arguments so that they turn into monster events;
- obsessively pursuing someone who is not really interested in an intimate relationship;
- trying to determine how much someone cares by fishing for compliments, sulking, nit-picking, or being surly and obnoxious;
- labeling your partner as bad and the relationship rotten based on a single unexpected or insensitive act;
- or settling for and staying in an unsatisfying relationship rather than acknowledging that a problem exists or taking steps to correct it.

Any relationship can include the recurring arguments, one-upmanship, jealousy, resentment, and sullen silence that results from thinking: I don't know what he wants from me, so I'll do anything *but* acknowledge my own feelings or reveal what I want from him. However, because you put all of you on the line in your intimate relationships, as did Jeff and Carol, baffling interactions involving your spouse or lover tend to be the most threatening and the most likely to trap you in a self-defeating pattern of mysterious moves and countermoves.

The Ultimate Consequence

Whether we pay the price in anxiety, stress, depression, work-related problems, or relationship conflicts, we ultimately discover the clear and ever-present danger of jumping to conclusions; *the mysteries we cannot solve come back to haunt us.*

For instance, Ralph, a successful thirty-five-year-old advertising executive, called in a favor in order to get his younger brother, Mark, a job interview with one of his clients. Although Mark, who had been unemployed for six months, told Ralph that the interview had gone well and that he was sure he would be offered the job, Ralph's client informed him that Mark was unprepared or unwilling to answer the interviewer's questions and didn't even have enough interest in the position to supply a résumé. When Ralph heard this, he became furious. He stormed around his office, cursing and grumbling, and then called his older sister to rant and rave about their brother. Ralph's sister, in turn, reported the entire conversation to their mother, who got angry and accused both siblings of having no compassion for their "poor" brother. Ralph's mother complained to his father, who appeared to take Ralph's side by asserting that his wife had always been partial to Mark and spoiled him. They argued and Ralph's father ended up blaming Ralph for creating the mess in the first place. Soon everyone in the family was at odds with everyone else, except for Mark, that is. He was left out of the turmoil entirely. This was precisely what had happened in this family countless times before. They had never figured out what went on below the surface in their family interactions, but whatever those mysterious forces were, they were still calling the shots.

Similarly, you may know one of the many men and women who embark upon new jobs with high hopes and grand expectations, only to become disillusioned within months, bitter and resistant within a year, apathetic and burned out the year after that. They then quit to take another job that they sincerely believe will fulfill their high hopes and grand expectations. Because the job is a factor, but not the whole issue, they invariably burn out again—generally in less time—and go looking for another "perfect" job which once again disappoints them.

Ralph's family and the idealistic job-switcher are living out the most universal and demoralizing unsolved mysteries of our lives: that whenever we operate with only part of the picture visible to us and jump to conclusions about the parts we cannot see, we set ourselves up to repeatedly re-experience that situation in some way, shape, or form. In fact, it sometimes seems as if once we encounter circumstances that baffle us, we cannot stop encountering them. We find ourselves:

- engaging in essentially the same arguments over and over again;
- ending one relationship only to begin another that soon seems remarkably and disturbingly like the first;
- surrounded by idiot supervisors, overbearing bosses, insubordinate subordinates and incompetent coworkers in every job we take;
- moving back and forth between opposite extremes—for example, trying to please and get along with everyone for a period of time, then resenting and switching to a "they can all go to hell" stance; or angrily snapping at our mothers, children, or spouses, then going to great lengths to make it up to them;
- ending up in one situation after another where we anxiously or helplessly ask ourselves—what's really going on here?

What You Don't Know *Can* Hurt You

Other unpleasant outcomes of jumping to conclusions about what is really going on in baffling situations include displacing your anger—taking out your frustration on the closest available target; being prone to emotional disorders, such as sudden angry outbursts, faulty judgment, panic attacks, burnout or defensive behavior; or developing a dependency on alcohol, drugs, food, work, gambling, sex or any other substance or activity that reduces anxiety, numbs unpleasant emotions or temporarily blocks out unsettling realities.

Please recognize that I am not saying that the inability to recognize and understand what is going on below the surface in various situations is the *only* or even the main reason that we experience these problems. However, after years of treating patients in my psychotherapy practice and studying human behavior in organizational and academic settings, I am convinced that there is indeed a direct and vital connection between the distressing circumstances I have described and our difficulties deciphering the secret code in which our own and other people's behavior is written. What we don't know *can* and often does hurt us.

Fortunately, there is a way to know more and hurt less, to crack the code and piece together the clues that can unravel the mysteries of everyday living. Our sleuthing begins with a deceptively simple concept, one which would no doubt prompt Sherlock Holmes to declare, "Elementary, my dear Watson": we do not always tell the truth, the whole truth, and nothing but the truth. We keep secrets instead.

2

The Truth and Nothing but the Truth? (Don't Bet on It)

Why We Keep Secrets from Ourselves and Others

Whenever you encounter baffling situations, the first question you ask yourself is What's really going on here? and the second is Why? *Why* does she have to be so secretive? *Why* did he lie about it? *Why* is he doing this to me? *Why* is he pretending that nothing's wrong when it's obvious that a crisis is brewing? *Why* didn't she tell me about this before I heard it from someone else? In the midst of a baffling interaction, such questions seem unanswerable. However, even though their objectives may not be readily apparent to you, nor yours to other people, there is always a reason for keeping secrets and incentives for not telling the truth, the whole truth, and nothing but the truth. They vary from individual to individual and from situation to situation, but tend to fall into one, two, or all three of the following categories:

- escaping pain: avoiding the negative consequences we fear will occur;
- seeking pleasure: obtaining positive rewards, immediate or long-term gratification of our needs and enhancement of our self-esteem;
- maintaining equilibrium: trying to ensure that external reality matches or at least approximates our internal perceptions of ourselves, other people, relationships, and specific situations.

Of these three, the most powerful motivation is escaping pain—physical or psychological pain, real or imagined pain, pain that we are experiencing at a given moment or pain that we anticipate feeling unless we do something to avoid it.

Secret Keeping for
Self-Protection

An instinct that dates back to primitive times when pain was a signal that your very survival was endangered, your desire to avoid pain takes precedence over all other motivations. You will forgo pleasure to escape pain. Higher-level needs and desires like learning or socializing are put on hold when you are in pain. And if you sense that something bad or painful is about to happen to you, honesty and communication fall by the wayside—which is clearly what happened to Seth and Abby, a couple who came to me for treatment shortly before I began working on this book.

Each year for the four years they have been married, Seth and Abby have exchanged Christmas gifts at midnight on Christmas Eve. This past Christmas they had put in such a full day that they could barely stay awake that long. They had gone to Seth's annual office party for employees and their families. Seth had dressed up as Santa Claus and Abby was not sure who was more delighted with the masquerade—the children whom Seth showered with attention, or Seth, who was aching to have children of his own. Then they had driven to Connecticut for dinner with Abby's family. Everyone had oohed and aahed over her older brother's new baby, and her younger sister had announced that she was pregnant—again. Tomorrow, they would go to Seth's parents' home for more of the same, and being a childless couple at Christmastime was taking its toll on both Seth (who wanted to start a family) and Abby (who said she wanted to have children, but actually did not).

Abby's career in banking was just beginning to take off, and unbeknown to Seth, she was up for a promotion that she very much wanted. What's more, she was not sure she would be happy living on Seth's salary alone, even temporarily. On two incomes they could afford the luxuries she had not had as the middle child of five in a family that barely made ends meet on the wages her father brought home from his factory job.

"My childhood was so crowded," she explained. "There was no place, no possession that was mine and mine alone. I know it sounds selfish, but I'm just not ready to share what we have with a child." Both because she did not like this "selfishness" in herself and because she did not think Seth would understand or accept her point of view, Abby did not reveal her true feelings to her husband. Instead, whenever the subject came up, she told Seth that she wanted to have children—but only when they could, as she put it, "do it right." She wanted to have a "real" home in the suburbs, she claimed, and enough financial security to be able to stay home to raise their children after they were born.

Seth sensed that Abby had more on her mind than houses and bank statements and thought he knew why. Remembering how reluctant she had been to marry him at all, and how they had dated for two years and lived together for three before she agreed, Seth thought: *It has more to do with me than money. She's still keeping her options open, making sure she doesn't get stuck with me because we have kids.* Seth never told Abby of this fear, although he felt it with full force each time they discussed starting a family.

After a year of anguishing over the matter, they had agreed to live less extravagantly in order to save money for a home and children. Seth saw this as a reasonable compromise. Abby viewed it as a sacrifice that she still was not sure she wanted to make. Although Abby had never actually complained about the change in lifestyle their arrangement precipitated, Seth got the message on Christmas Eve. Under the tissue paper of a long, flat box he had assumed contained gloves or a necktie, Seth found two airline tickets to Hawaii and a brochure describing the resort where Abby had made reservations for the two of them. He was shocked by the extravagance of Abby's gift and its apparent meaning.

He thought: *This clinches it. She isn't the least bit interested in having children. If she was, she wouldn't have blown her whole year-end bonus on a trip to Hawaii. She doesn't care about me or what I want at all.*

Not wanting to hurt Abby or start an argument at midnight on Christmas Eve, in spite of the devastating conclusion he had drawn, Seth forced a smile and mustered as much enthusiasm as he could. "A trip to Hawaii!" he exclaimed.

"This is great. What a surprise!" As valiant an effort as this was, Seth could not disguise his dismay.

Abby thought: *Uh-oh. He's upset. I guess I should have known he would be. But it was such a huge bonus and we haven't taken a real vacation in so long . . . Oh God, he wants children so much. But what am I supposed to do? If I don't agree to have kids I'll lose him and be miserable, but if I do, I'll be just as miserable.*

Torn and terrified, Abby began to cry. "I'm sorry about the present," she sobbed. "I'm sorry I can't give you what you want."

Seth was hit with a wave of sheer panic.

What is she saying? Is she crying because I wasn't thrilled with her gift or because she's about to tell me she doesn't want kids at all, ever, and maybe doesn't want to be married anymore either? Oh God, what if that is what she means?

Seth was not about to ask. Instead, he employed a maneuver that I call Jumping the Gun: to ensure that he "heard" something that he could handle and *not* what he was afraid Abby would say, Seth, without waiting or trying to find out what might really be going on, replaced what he was afraid was going on with a less threatening explanation for Abby's tears.

He thought: *She's been working really hard, and between my one-track mind and hearing about kids all the time because it's Christmas, she must be completely stressed out. She must really need a vacation right now, a break from all the pressure about money and starting a family. Maybe I can take the pressure off. . . .*

Jumping the gun to fix what he had decided was broken, Seth said, "I know you really want to go on this vacation, and I think you should do it, but maybe you should go by yourself. I mean, you're probably pretty sick of me and all my baby talk anyway, and since I can't really take any time off from work right now . . ."

Although Seth continued to talk, Abby could not hear him over the roar of her own panic-stricken thoughts:

What is he trying to tell me? Doesn't he want to be with me? Have I lost him already?

As you might expect, Seth and Abby's discussion did not end here. Indeed it went round and round for hours. In a conversation full of secrecy, each in his or her own way grappled with the four interconnected issues that all of us devote at least some of our attention to during any meaningful interaction:

1. how we perceive ourselves ("I know I sound selfish," Abby said);
2. how the other person perceives us *(She doesn't care about me or what I want,* Seth thought);
3. how we perceive the other person (Seth and Abby each believed that the other person was on the verge of leaving);
4. what we want from the interaction or relationship (which was, of course, the most crucial issue to Seth and Abby during the encounter I just described).

If, based on the subtlest signal, the slightest niggling doubt, we sense that we are about to think less of ourselves; cause the other person to think less of us; think less of and thus be unable to get along with the other person; or get something that we do *not* want from the interaction, we become anxious and upset. Internal voices begin to bombard us with words of warning, reminders of the pain and other negative consequences we might suffer. The other person might reject or disapprove of us, seize anything we "give away" and use it against us. We might have to face our own shortcomings and feel inadequate or unlovable; or fail to live up to our own or other people's expectations, proving that we really are not good enough managers, parents, spouses, friends, or lovers. What if we end up having an argument, hurting someone's feelings, losing our job, or unleashing a flood of negative emotions like anger and being unable to regain our composure? The number of potential catastrophes we can conjure up in our minds is limitless and they all lead to the same conclusion. *I am going to get hurt,* we think, *and I can't let that happen.* So we protect ourselves by keeping certain facts or feelings hidden.

This is not a character defect, but rather a coping strategy that will at times work in your best interest. Indeed, the following *defensive maneuvers* have probably gotten you out of many anxiety-provoking or emotionally distressing situations in the past, and chances are that you still use them on a regular basis.

DEFENSIVE MANEUVERS

Lies, Half-truths, Omissions, and Cover-ups

When you believe that telling the truth, the whole truth, and nothing but the truth will hurt you in some way, you will conceal, camouflage, or misrepresent reality by telling anything from a complete untruth ("Nobody told me there was a meeting today") to a little white lie ("I thought your presentation was fascinating"). You may tell half-truths—"I couldn't get it done because the copier broke down" (for thirty minutes five hours ago)—or simply say nothing at all about a particular event.

In spite of the fact that most of us were raised to value honesty highly, defensive maneuvers such as lies, half-truths, omissions, and cover-ups tend to be the ones we turn to first and employ most frequently. Under certain circumstances, they are viable options—which is not to say that you should lie your way out of sticky situations, but rather acknowledge the way things are in the real world. When complete honesty could cause more harm than good, lying is one alternative available to you and sometimes you will decide—hopefully after careful, conscious consideration—that it is the one you will use.

Of course, this defensive maneuver has the potential to create as many problems as it helps you avoid. For one thing, you always run the risk of getting caught in your lies and winding up with a much bigger mess and a good deal more explaining to do than you would have been faced with originally, or you may expend valuable time and energy worrying —wondering if other people believed your story or only pretended to, keeping a watchful eye on everything you say or do, trying to keep your stories straight and so on.

What's more, you participate in elaborate cover-ups to make sure that no one discovers a secret that could be damaging to you, but your anxiety about possibly letting something slip, along with any guilt you might feel about having told a big or little lie in the first place, frequently strains your relationships with the people from whom you are keeping secrets.

Deflection

- "You're just jealous."
- "There you go, blowing things out of proportion again."
- "You're not exactly Mr. Efficiency yourself."

Whenever your first response to a statement made about you has an accusatory "you" in it, chances are that you are defending yourself against the negative implications of the message you just received. To take the heat off yourself, you use the defensive maneuver of deflection, focusing on the other person's "bad" behavior so that you don't have to examine or acknowledge your own inappropriate actions.

You may also deflect comments that are unacceptable to

you by critiquing the comment itself. For example, imagine a coworker who shares your office saying, "You really have to get organized. Just look at this desk—files everywhere, notes to yourself on scraps of paper, computer printouts with coffee stains all over them and crumpled wrappers from everything you ate this week. How can you get your work done in this mess?" In response, you might attempt to:

- prove that the statement is wrong based on faulty logic ("There is no evidence that people with messy desks are less organized or efficient than people with neat ones.");
- trivialize it ("So my desk is a mess. If that's the worst you have to say about me, I must be doing okay.");
- ignore it;
- question the speaker's motives ("My desk is always a mess. What's the big deal today? Must be that the boss is stopping by and you want to impress him.").

Deflection is a tactic that is particularly useful for countering your fear that your own shortcomings will be your undoing. It allows you to get the message and then immediately get rid of it without thinking less of yourself or feeling anxious, sad, inadequate, or embarrassed.

Having a Problem That Isn't the Real Problem

"He did it again," the secretary said to no one in particular. Anyone in the employee lunchroom of the office-supply company was free to respond. A billing clerk, seated nearby, did.

"Who?" she asked.

"Allen," the secretary began, and everyone in the room either groaned or shook his head. Allen was always doing something. In a matter of moments, a spirited discussion that might be titled "The Trouble with Allen," is off and running. Allen is "the worst" about paperwork. He turns in illegible expense reports whenever he feels like it, instead of once a month as he is supposed to. He promises customers things he can't deliver and then they get angry at his supervisor for setting the record straight. He thinks he can "sweet talk" people into doing things for him and everyone swears that the only way he can close a sale is by wining and dining and probably having sex with office managers and secretaries all over town. Everyone has something to say. "Really," they agree. "Someone should do something about Allen."

However, if someone really did do something about Allen, chances are that these disgruntled employees would find someone or something else to complain about in much the same way. They need Allen—or another problem that is not the real problem—both as a rallying point that unifies them and as a defense against more threatening forces, including the many unalterable sources of dissatisfaction that come from working for a company that demands a great deal from its workers but seems to give them little in return.

Almost every office, factory, committee, or classroom, as well as many couples and families, has an individual or issue they blame for most if not all of their problems. In addition to creating a sense of belonging based on an "us against them" mentality, scapegoating, like deflection, directs our attention away from more anxiety-provoking and intractable problems.

For instance, you may know a married couple whose relationship is always on the rocks, and from watching and listening to them it may seem obvious that there is a fundamental problem in that relationship—incompatible expectations, for example, poor communication, lack of trust, possessiveness, more interest in their careers than their marriage or something along those lines. Yet they may appear completely oblivious to the facts that are so apparent to you. "We're just going through a rough time now," they might say. "Everything will be fine once Joe gets a better job, or Mary gets pregnant, or we buy a house." Or they might blame their problems on their meddling in-laws, their financial status or their hyperactive child. Yet, when one outside problem gets solved, another one always seems to pop up to take its place. "There's always something," they chuckle and go right on bickering, making sarcastic comments to each other, or barely speaking to one another.

As with that couple, when we use this maneuver we do not have to acknowledge or feel its full impact. Instead we hide our thoughts, feelings, and unmet needs behind a readily identifiable problem, direct our anger and frustration at it, and channel our energy into solving it. Our real issues never get resolved, of course. And we are apt to feel more confused and powerless than ever. But we do not realize this while it is happening.

Creating Distance

"Sometimes I feel like I'm living with a complete stranger," Diana, a forty-year-old mother of three, commented on the recent and dramatic changes in her relationship with her six-teen-year-old daughter, Ellen. "It's as if one night while she was sleeping, an entirely different person slipped in and possessed her body. She looks like my daughter. Every once in a while she acts like my daughter, but most of the time she is someone I barely recognize—a moody, distant, uncommunicative alien being.

"We used to talk all the time about everything." Diana sighed. "I knew what Ellen was thinking and feeling. Now I'm lucky to hear three complete sentences from her in a single day. The answer to every question is 'I don't know. Nothing. Nowhere. Get off my back.' She's just so damn secretive these days and that worries me. What if she's in some kind of trouble but isn't telling me?"

Although it upsets Diana, who worries about what Ellen is keeping from her and misses the close relationship she used to have with her daughter, Ellen is simply doing what all teenagers do—developing an individual identity—in the same way most adolescents do it—by controlling what and how much information about herself and her activities she reveals to her parents.

Long after adolescence we keep secrets for similar reasons. We construct boundaries to define where we end and other people begin, to reinforce our sense of being separate and distinct human beings. What's more, whenever we sense that those boundaries are about to be violated—that our privacy, autonomy or freedom to control our own lives is being threatened—we employ a defensive maneuver that I call creating distance. We change the subject when a conversation is hitting too close to home; make jokes during serious or tender moments; keep ourselves too busy to deal with emotional issues; do not listen; do not talk; start arguments—usually at inopportune moments and often right before bedtime; or seduce the partner who seems to be pushing for more closeness—both to interrupt a threatening interaction and because we hope that physical intimacy will temporarily satisfy our partner's desire for emotional intimacy.

We almost always create distance between ourselves and people who we perceive to be more powerful than we are—and who actually may be by virtue of their position in relation to us. We keep parents, teachers, bosses, and other authority figures from having too much control or controlling certain areas of our lives simply by keeping them at arm's length and making sure they do not know everything that is going on.

Secrets Can Also
Be Power Plays

Although secret keeping is most likely to be a defensive maneuver to get less of what we don't want, it can also be used to get more of what we need, want, or believe we deserve. Rather than quaking in our boots and building a barrier to protect us from the negative consequences we fear, we can flex our muscles and remove any obstacles that stand between us and something that would bring us pleasure. By carefully controlling the amount and kind of information we reveal, we engage in power plays that, if successful, get other people to do what we want them to do without figuring out what we are up to.

Button Pushing

"Haven't I always supported you?" a marketing director says to one of his account executives, a young woman whom he mentored since she began working for the company as a receptionist. "I've been in your corner every time you've had a problem. Nobody has as much faith in you as I do." Although it may sound as if the director is reassuring her of his backing, he is actually manipulating her. She has come into his office to confront him about assigning to another account executive a project she developed and his exploiting her sense of gratitude and obligation so that she will drop a subject he prefers not to discuss.

"Well, if you can't handle it . . . I mean, it is a lot of responsibility . . ." a supervisor says to a worker who prides himself on being responsible. By thus implying that the worker does not have what it takes to do the job, the supervisor increases the likelihood that the worker will accept an assignment that should not be his responsibility in the first place and which he has every right to turn down.

"It's okay. I understand how busy you are. You have your priorities." *And I'm not one of them*—is the implied message conveyed by one friend trying to manipulate another into meeting for lunch.

The account executive, the achievement-oriented employee, and the friend have just had their "buttons" pushed. They have had their sore spots, vulnerabilities, or insecurities exploited by a power player who knows precisely how to stir up anxiety, confusion, frustration, and defensiveness. Losing their objectivity, they automatically do whatever it takes to appease or protect themselves from the manipulator—which is exactly what the manipulator hoped they would do.

Parents can be expert button pushers. "Do I really ask that much of you?" they inquire. "Am I really that much of a burden? Did you hear me complaining when I was _____ [fill in the blank with anything from paying for your college education to changing your dirty diapers]." Guardians of "the right thing to do," our parents can use variations on this theme to guilt us into doing almost anything. What's more, in spite of having promised ourselves that we never would, we push our children's and other people's guilt buttons too. It really is one of the quickest, easiest, most surefire ways to get other people to do what we want them to do.

In addition, we push our spouse's and lover's "If you really cared, you would . . ." buttons; our staff's "Are you as competent as you think you are?" buttons; our boss's "Are you really in control of this situation?" buttons, to name a few. By doing so, we create a state of psychological distress which others can remedy only by giving us what we want or need.

Of course, button pushing requires a certain amount of finesse and is in fact a very risky venture. If your victim recognizes that you are using this power play while it is in use (as opposed to figuring it out when it is too late to do anything about it), the tactic not only fails but can lead to, or escalate, a bitter conflict or confrontation. For this reason, most of us combine button pushing with other strategies, including the next one.

Softening Them Up for the Kill

This power play involves getting people to trust, like, and feel comfortable with you so they will *want* to do whatever you ask of them. There are many ways we may go about softening people up for the kill. We may flatter, commiserate, reveal what appear to be intimate details about ourselves, share confidential information about other people or about "top secret" upcoming events, ask for their advice, tell a hard-luck story or otherwise convey the impression that we respect, admire, like, and know we can count on them. Won over by our maneuvers, they let down their guard, and motivated by their desire to maintain the special relationship with us, they become more willing to meet our needs. Having softened them up, we then move in for the kill, using a direct or indirect approach to get what we wanted all along—an employee to do something that is not in his or her job description, for instance; a reluctant partner to have sex with you; or your parents to go easy on you for buying yourself an expensive gift with their credit card.

Like most power plays, softening people up for the kill is dangerous. It does indeed work from time to time and is not transparent enough for people to see through and choose not to buy into. However, when this power play backfires, it destroys trust and creates the suspicion that every kind or friendly act on your part is insincere.

Setups and Mixed Messages

Setups and mixed messages include pouting; giving people the silent treatment; asking questions we have already answered for ourselves or which other people cannot answer without telling us what we want to hear; nonverbal signals that contradict our words; or making comparisons in hopes of getting one person to be more like another. These power plays are both common and effective and can be remarkably subtle. We can use them to obtain comfort or reassurance without actually asking for the attention we crave, or to regain the advantage over someone who has gotten one up on us—which is what Jane, the mother who "knew" she was right about the oven temperature, did.

Expecting her daughter Sara to acknowledge and appreciate that, as her mother, she knew more about certain things and was the ultimate authority in certain areas, she set Sara up by asking a question. Then when she did not get the answer she wanted ("You're right, Mom. It is set too high"), she sent a mixed message (saying she trusted Sara's judgment, but nonverbally signaling the opposite). Although Jane never actually got Sara to concede that she was more knowledgeable about cooking and thus turn down the oven temperature, she still came out the winner. When Sara overreacted to her mother's hidden agenda and reverted to the role of a child throwing a tantrum, Jane was able to confirm that she was still the more mature, rational, in-control person in their relationship—which was more or less what she wanted all along.

In addition, because these maneuvers often enrage other people, we get an excuse to vent our own anger, outrage, or resentment. If they get angry first, we think we are justified in getting angry in response, and for many of us those are the only circumstances in which we feel comfortable expressing anger. What's more, setups and mixed messages come with built in self-protective shields. If we get caught in the act, we maintain the upper hand by denying that we did what we did (or that we intended to). "I just wanted what was best for you," we claim. "I was only trying to help," we insist. "I don't know what you're so worked up about," we say.

Setups and mixed messages can also be used punitively. As Kate did, we can subtly and sometimes not so subtly signal that we are upset or angry, implying that the person receiving the signal is the source of our discontent but not specifying the actual misdeed they committed. Or operating from a "misery loves company" stance, we can make the other person as miserable as we are by withholding information (or affection), "forgetting" to do something we were asked to do, sulking, "accidentally" bringing up a topic we know the other person is sensitive about, going over our supervisor's head to complain to his supervisor, or in some other ingenious way "making them pay" for what we believe they have done to us.

Creating an Impression

When you want to be liked by or fit in with other people, you engage in a variety of relatively benign deceptions that leave others with a more positive impression of you. For instance, you may pretend to agree with people whose positive regard you cherish or you may claim to have no opinion on the topic being discussed by a group whose acceptance is important to you. You may choose not to mention your marital or work-related problems to a friend because you do not want to impose. Or you might tell your spouse, lover, children, or coworkers that everything is going to be okay—even though you are as sure as they are that it will not. Your motives are about as altruistic as they will ever get. You are keeping secrets to protect someone you care about from a painful truth or to help them feel better about themselves. Of course, it does not hurt that they feel better about it and like you more in return.

In addition, we recommend restaurants, books, and movies in hopes of getting closer to someone by sharing our experiences with them. We readily reveal our opinions on the best wine, cars, personal computers, and preschools to impress other people with our sophistication; or offer tips on how to cook a gourmet dish, remove a stain, or organize files in order to impress them with our knowledge. In short, we make a good many seemingly innocuous statements for motives that go beyond simply holding up our end of the conversation. We want the pleasure of this other person's friendship, respect, or admiration and we use a variety of subtle strategic maneuvers as a means toward that end.

Power Plays Are a
Means to an End

What is the incentive for engaging in hidden agenda power plays? The second of the three basic motivations for human behavior—seeking pleasure. Even though we may not be particularly proud of the means we use to obtain it, the end result—being liked because of the impression we made, confirming our ability to control others, getting even, receiving reassurance, or simply amassing power for its own sake—feels good. In fact, although we hate it when people use power plays on us, we rarely regret having used one ourselves—if it works, that is. A power play that fails is apt to infuriate or frustrate us to no end.

Of course, if we are in a position of authority or if the

other person already believes that *not* complying with our wishes will hurt them, we could achieve our goals by using a more direct approach. This is why those of us who are in less powerful, one-down positions are most likely to rely on power plays to get our own way as well as to combat the power imbalance in any situation or relationship. Sometimes the only way we can win is to conceal the fact that we are playing at all. Or as one of my patients put it, "I can get my husband to do anything I want. All I have to do is convince him that he's the one who thought of it."

Of course, I do not want to overlook the fact that those of us who already have a certain amount of power, and especially those of us whose self-esteem rests on exercising our power over others, enjoy getting other people to give us what we want without their figuring out what we are up to. Keeping secrets allows us to win at a more complicated and challenging game, to feel more powerful because we have gotten our own way without giving ourselves away.

Maintaining the Status Quo

The final incentive for secret keeping is our innate desire to maintain our equilibrium; to ensure that what goes on around us remains consistent and harmonious with our internal view of the way we, other people, and life as a whole are supposed to be. When maintaining the status quo is our motive, controlling the flow of information helps us:

- think, feel, and behave in ways that are consistent with our self-concept;
- make sure that other people do not change their opinions of us;
- hang on to our images of other people, as idealized or unrealistic as they may be;

- ensure that various situations and relationships remain as stable and predictable as possible.

The maneuvers that maintain the status quo are those that don't rock the boat or will enable us to push unpleasant thoughts to the back of our minds because "thinking about it only makes matters worse." They are products of the psychological version of the physical law of inertia—even when where we are is not good for us, it is easier to stay put than to change ourselves or our situation.

Consequently, much of the secret keeping we do in the name of maintaining equilibrium has us knowingly deceiving ourselves. We encounter situations in which something—be it a tyrannical boss, a vindictive coworker, an unmotivated child, a nosy neighbor, or our own self-defeating habits—disturbs us, but we cannot or are not ready to resolve the problem. Since there is nothing we can do about it and since it won't go away, we find some way to disguise it. This makes distressing events and relationships seem less distressing, but only temporarily. As you may know from your own experience with them, even though we use conscious self-deceptions on a regular basis, they are not particularly effective. In fact, we generally have to repeat them to ourselves each time an unpleasant reality arises or periodically replace them with more elaborate explanations.

Nonacceptance

When the disturbing conversation with her teenaged son's guidance counselor finally ends, Mary replaces the telephone receiver and shakes her head in disbelief. "There must be some explanation," she says, "some mistake. My son would not participate in destruction of school property. I raised him better than that."

"I can't believe he didn't call," Ellie says to her co-worker on Thursday morning. "He didn't say 'I'll give you a call sometime,' the way a lot of men do. He made it very clear that he would call on Wednesday night. He seemed like such a nice guy too. I just can't believe I was wrong about him."

"That won't happen," Bill, a forty-year-old stockbroker, said to a colleague who had just told him about the tip he had received from someone in management. The tipster's advice was to look for employment elsewhere, because the staff was going to be cut back 75 percent. "I know times are tough right now, but the market will pick up," the broker continued. "This is a big company. It should be able to weather this crisis without taking such drastic measures. Besides, after all I've put into this company, they'd never do something like that to me." He continued to tell himself this right up until he was called into his boss's office and told that he was being let go.

"He wouldn't do that," "I can't believe it," "This isn't happening"—those are the sounds of nonacceptance. Of course, whatever is disturbing you is indeed happening and you know it. You are aware of the facts and your feelings, but you *do not want to be.* And so, instead of asking yourself what the circumstances mean to you and what you can do about them, you declare your disbelief as if that somehow dismisses or decides the matter. Oh, you may vent your outrage and frustration or automatically compensate for your feelings by soliciting advice from friends but not really listening to it, "tying one on," or working out more vigorously than usual. You may even obsess about the situation. But you do not *accept* the reality or its implications and you consciously choose not to deal with it.

Of course, deciding not to accept something does not make it go away or prevent it from affecting you, which is why you are apt rather quickly to move on to some other self-deception maneuver, such as:

- **Distortion:** explaining away a reality in order to maintain your illusion. For instance Mary, whose son destroyed school property, might tell herself, "I don't have to deal with this because it was just a one-time thing. He'll never do it again." Or Ellie, who did not receive the phone call she expected, might say, "Maybe he meant next Wednesday."

- **Distraction:** channeling your energy into unrelated activities. Whether you exercise, meditate, go to the movies, or refinish furniture, this tactic works if you actually allow yourself to be distracted and truly focus your attention on what you are doing. It is useful and in your best interest only if you are fully aware that you are temporarily distracting yourself. Automatic habitual distractions—from overeating to indiscriminate sexual activity—can end up controlling rather than comforting you.

- **Compensation:** This self-deception is used to deal with mixed emotions—especially when you believe that you should not be feeling one of them. For example, a newly promoted executive may tell anyone who will listen how wonderful the job is, never once mentioning how exhausting or stressful it is. Or a man who is grateful to his in-laws for their financial support, but finds them irritating and at times obnoxious, may go out of his way to be kind to them and include them in as many family activities as possible. Both are knowingly and intentionally compensating for their own ambivalence by overexpressing or overdramatizing one side of the issue and ignoring the other, generally negative, side.

Suppression

During the course of certain therapy sessions, I, like all psychotherapists, sometimes notice that something going on in that session has triggered my personal agenda, stirring up thoughts and feelings that are attached to my own personal experiences. As a result, I may experience an impulse to shut down and not listen or use some consoling platitude like "Every cloud has a silver lining." However, neither of these responses would be either appropriate or helpful to my patient. If I cannot make use of my own agenda on behalf of my patient at that time, I temporarily put those thoughts and feelings on hold, using a method I adapted from one of my training supervisors. I conjure up an image of an empty chair and seat whatever I want to put on hold in that chair. In my mind, I say to my anger, frustration, anxiety, or rescue fantasy, "I hear you. Now, sit here and be quiet. I'll get back to you later." And that statement is an example of *suppression.*

Suppression involves consciously rejecting a thought or feeling *for the time being;* holding in an emotion until you are safely able to express and deal with it or the situation that is causing it. You quickly push unpleasant facts and feelings to the back of your mind or replace them with other thoughts when you:

- have other, more pressing matters to attend to;
- are already emotionally overloaded or physically exhausted;
- are too angry to think clearly;
- recognize that the person who is upsetting you is in no condition to discuss the problem;
- don't have enough information about a situation to decide how to handle it;

- don't trust your own interpretation and want to talk things over with a therapist, friend, family member, or coworker;
- realize that your anxious or negative thoughts and feelings are getting in your way—preventing you from fulfilling other aspects of your psychological agenda.

Under these circumstances, it is apt to be in your best interest *not* to face or do anything about the situation you have encountered. Suppression serves as a temporary stopgap measure. It gives you an opportunity to calm down, cool off, get your job done, and handle crises without falling to pieces. You come back later to the thoughts and feelings you suppressed and both deal with and learn from them, asking yourself, "What did this situation tell me about myself, other people, and this particular interaction? What am I going to do with this new information? How can I prepare myself for similar situations and be able to handle things differently in the future?"

Unfortunately, for many of us suppression becomes a way of life instead of a short-term maneuver. We push down our thoughts and feelings every time they come up and expend valuable energy on one attempt after another *not* to accept reality. The emotions we bottle up clamor to be released like steam in a pressure cooker. They seep out in a variety of ways, sometimes physically, contributing to ulcers, headaches, frequent colds, physical exhaustion, and other stress-related ailments. And sometimes they explode, causing the sort of overreaction Sara had. Having spent a week swallowing her resentment of her mother's "helpful hints" and thinly disguised criticisms, every last drop of anger surged to the surface over the admittedly trivial matter of the oven temperature setting.

The great fallacy of the last decade was, If I have an

emotion, I must express it. The fact is that doing and saying exactly what you are thinking or feeling is not necessarily good for you in every situation you encounter. But neither is keeping secrets. The tactics I have described in this chapter can be adaptive and useful, and in your best interests at least some of the time. However, they can also be overused, used in situations where a more direct approach is warranted, or used in situations without thinking about the repercussions that they have on us, others, or our relationships.

Are the defensive maneuvers, power plays, or self-deceptions you use working for you or against you? The following self-awareness exercise will help you find out.

The Secret-
Keeping Self-test
—

Although you have no doubt employed each of these tactics at least once, chances are that you turn to certain maneuvers more than others and use several of them on a fairly regular basis. Flipping back through this chapter or referring to the glossary on page 241, identify the secret-keeping methods you are most likely to use.

Then think about a recent incident or interaction in which you used one or more of those approaches.

How much of what you wanted did you actually get? (Mark the point between the two extremes that most closely represents your answer.)

ALL   **NONE**

How much of what you *feared* would happen did you actually prevent from happening?

ALL   **NONE**

In terms of actually solving the problem or settling matters, how successful was your approach? (COMPLETELY SUCCESSFUL—totally solved or settled with nothing remotely resembling those circumstances ever arising again. COMPLETELY UNSUCCESSFUL—nothing solved or settled and the conflict escalating or arising repeatedly.)

COMPLETELY SUCCESSFUL   **COMPLETELY UNSUCCESSFUL**

In terms of its impact on you, others, or your ongoing relationship, how beneficial was your approach? (EXTREMELY BENEFICIAL—enhanced self-esteem, improved communication, and strengthened your relationship. DEVASTATING—one or both parties hurt, demeaned, or diminished, lines of communication shut down, relationship damaged possibly beyond repair.)

EXTREMELY BENEFICIAL   **DEVASTATING**

If your marks fell to the right of center on one or more of these continuums, your maneuver clearly did *not* work in your best interest in that particular situation. If your marks fell to the left of center, if you got most or all of what you wanted, managed to ward off the consequences you feared, settled the matter and benefited from the interaction, the tactic *may have* served you. I emphasized the words "may have" because there are still several factors to consider before concluding that your deceptive approach actually worked.

Regardless of the outcome, in the aftermath of your maneuver did you or others suffer negative repercussions such as:

- guilt;
- resentment;
- additional confusion;
- self-doubt;
- anger (expressed openly or covertly);
- anxiety;
- repeatedly replaying the entire incident in your mind;
- reviewing what you or they could have or should have done and criticizing them or yourself for being too stupid and bullheaded or mean-spirited to do the right thing;
- the compelling urge to go back and explain, apologize, or give that person a piece of your mind;
- the desire to tell a third party about what happened in hopes of being reassured that you handled the situation appropriately?

Did tension remain in the air for several hours or several days after the incident or interaction took place?

Did people directly involved in or directly aware of the incident seem to distance themselves from you by actually walking away, diverting their gaze, discontinuing conversations when you approached, or being less friendly than they had been in the past?

Was there more turmoil after the incident than there had been before? Did friends, relatives, or colleagues gossip about the incident, choose sides, put their two cents in, or otherwise get involved?

After the fact, did others intimate that the approach you used in that situation was one they had seen you use many times before? Did they seem to insinuate that it made no sense to them or got on their nerves? Did you think:

- There they go again, getting angry at me for no reason.
- They're always criticizing, nit-picking, nagging.

• Why is everyone hassling me to get into therapy, read some dumb self-help book, or change a perfectly harmless little habit?

When any of the above occurs, secret keeping is not working in your best interest. Even if you are getting or avoiding most or all of what you wanted, you are paying too high a price.

This is apt to be the case whenever you:

• use the same tactic in many different situations;
• use the same tactics over and over again even though they do not provide the results you desire;
• use them even though you have only a vague notion of what you are thinking, feeling, or hoping to accomplish.

Why would you do these things and why do other people repeatedly seem to use the same costly secret-keeping strategies on you? Because you and everyone around you are trying to fulfill a psychological agenda: the internal list of needs, wants, wishes, and expectations each of us carries at all times and uses to guide our actions in any situation or relationship.

3

Agendas You See, Agendas You Don't

What Makes
Our Agendas Open,
Hidden, or Automatic

According to Kate—the wife who gave her husband the silent treatment in Chapter 1—the day of her telephone call to Michael had been a horror show. The magazine's managing editor had shot down in an instant a story idea that had required a great deal of time and energy to develop. A writer "freaked out" when Kate called her to ask for revisions. And worst of all, she had received a disturbing letter from her mother.

"I felt awful," Kate confessed. "Like the whole world was against me and I needed to know that Michael was on my side. I just needed a little sympathy—and he hung up on me instead."

As Kate finished her last sentence, Michael, who had

been listening intently and with compassion, pulled back and defensively folded his arms across his chest. "How was I supposed to know what you needed?" he snapped. "You didn't say a word about it."

Indeed, she did not. She kept secrets instead. She concealed her true feelings under a subterfuge of small talk and questions about how *his* day was going—hoping that he would, in turn, ask about *her* day or eventually respond to one of the hints she would have dropped if their conversation had lasted longer.

"I was already feeling so needy and insecure," she explained. "I hate feeling that way and if I just came out and told him I was upset, it would have made things worse. I would have felt like I was begging. But if Michael had *asked* what was wrong, well, things would have been okay then. I would have known that he wasn't just pretending that he cared because I asked him to."

Kate's feelings of insecurity and neediness, her desire to be comforted by her husband and her determination not to beg for attention were all elements of her *psychological agenda* —the internal outline of needs, wants, wishes, and expectations she hoped to fulfill during her conversation with Michael. That agenda determined both what Kate wanted to get from the interaction and how she tried to get it.

Like Kate, each of us does what we do, thinks what we think, and feels what we feel based on our psychological agendas—agendas that organize everything we have learned in the past, influence our perceptions of what is or should be happening in the present, and keep track of our hopes for the future. All of us, without exception, have psychological agendas and need them. Our lives would be completely unmanageable without them—a crazy quilt of meaningless memories, scattered thoughts, random feelings, and disconnected images. Nothing would make sense to us. Like those outlines that organize the topics to be covered in a board meeting or set forth what we hope to accomplish at a sales conference, our psychological agendas guide us through the varied and complex interactions that are part and parcel of our daily lives and relationships.

No matter what you do, where you do it, or with whom, at the most fundamental level you are always trying to fulfill your agenda, to meet the needs and expectations it contains—and so are all of the people around you.

Of course, there is no guarantee that the needs, fears, and wishes found in other people's agendas will even remotely resemble, much less match, your own. Psychological agendas are as unique to an individual as his or her own fingerprints. They are one-of-a-kind patchwork quilts pieced together from the life experiences you have accumulated and interpreted in your own way. As a result, while your own and other people's perceptions and expectations for a given situation may be complementary, compatible, or even exactly the same, you and others will not think, feel, and act in precisely the same way in all situations.

In addition, items on your own and other people's agendas can conflict so that meeting your needs prevents someone else from meeting his or vice versa. For instance, Kate needed Michael to hang on the phone until he figured out that she was upset and wanted comforting, but Michael needed to get off the phone and meet with his boss, so an agenda conflict occurred. Clearly both could not get what they needed from that particular situation. A battle of the wills was inevitable. When such a battle occurs, the person who is able to fulfill his agenda wins while the person whose needs go unmet loses—and none of us likes to lose. In fact, the mere prospect of losing sends us into a tailspin—adding an emotional charge to an already baffling situation.

Of course, when other people's agendas do not match or in fact conflict with our own, we could open-mindedly negotiate compromises. Or at least we could if we knew what those agendas were. But as you know, by choice or habit we do not straightforwardly convey our needs and expectations to others. Neither do they reveal their agendas to us. In fact, during most human interactions and virtually all baffling ones, you and other people use not just one, but three psychological agendas—and two of the three are invisible to the naked eye.

- **Open** agendas contain the needs, feelings, and expectations that you are aware of yourself and convey to others directly. They can tell the whole story or represent just the tip of the iceberg.

- **Hidden** agendas are the wishes, hopes, desires, and assumptions that you recognize in yourself, but choose to conceal or camouflage during your interactions with other people. They operate just below the surface and are responsible for the inconsistencies and ulterior motives that you sense in others but cannot accurately identify or fully understand.

- **Automatic** agendas, comprised of the needs, drives, emotions, and motives that you do *not* consciously recognize or understand in yourself, are underneath it all. These truly baffling elements, which you could not explain to others even if you wanted to, dramatically influence your thoughts, feelings, and actions and are responsible for the lion's share of your own and other people's most bewildering, habitual behaviors.

Open Agendas

Several hours after his disconcerting encounter with Eddie, Barry brought his secretary, Helen, a memo to type and circulate. "Could you get to this right away?" he asked.

"Right away, right away—or right away after the meeting minutes you wanted me to type right away?" Helen inquired.

Barry paused to think about Helen's question and then replied, "The memo first, then the minutes."

"Will do," she said, took the page she had been working on out of the typewriter, inserted a clean sheet of stationery, and began to type.

When Barry walked away from this interaction, he did not wonder what was really going on. No feelings of anxiety, frustration, or self-doubt churned inside him. He did not spend a single second of his time worrying about what he should have done differently or devising a plan to do things another way in the future. He did not have to. In that particular situation, both he and Helen operated with *open agendas.*

As simple and perhaps even simplistic as this example may seem, the encounter could have proceeded quite differently, since Barry did have a rather irritating habit of saying, "Can you get to this right away?" each and every time he gave Helen something to do. Consequently, Helen might have taken the memo from him and typed it immediately, grumbling the entire time and making herself miserable. She might have assumed that right away meant as soon as she could get to it, setting it aside only to have Barry criticize her when he came looking for it a short time later. Or she might have "accidentally" misplaced it or forgotten about it or intentionally set it aside, telling herself that she would get to it when she was "good and ready." She could even have been hostile toward Barry. But instead of reacting in any of these ways, Helen chose to use an open agenda. She needed to know what Barry wanted her to do first, so she asked him.

Similarly, the interaction might have created emotional fallout for Helen if Barry had *not* answered her directly. If he had said, "Whatever you think," or shrugged or made a vague comment like, "Just get to it as soon as you can," Helen would have been left to guess what he really wanted. Not only would this have annoyed her, but if she "guessed" wrong, Barry would have been angry about it or at least inconvenienced. Then she might have stewed resentfully because her boss was making her miserable or berated herself for being too dumb to figure out what he really meant. Fortunately, Barry also used an open agenda and answered Helen's question in a forthright manner.

Asking the question you need answered, as Helen did; choosing the option that is in your best interest and conveying that preference, as Barry did; expressing an opinion; laughing when something strikes you as funny; telling your spouse that you need help cleaning out the attic; crying when you feel sad; asking your son to arrange for someone else to drive him to little league because you have to work late, are all examples of open agendas in action. You can tell because what you do and say is consistent with what you think and feel. You recognize what you need from a situation or another person and you go about meeting that need *directly.*

Sometimes this involves saying exactly what you mean. "I told her I was busy and I couldn't talk," Michael explained earlier. He was using an open agenda. Sometimes it entails simply doing what you truly want to do—like unplugging the telephone and taking a hot bath when you feel frazzled or ordering a pizza instead of preparing dinner when you don't feel like cooking. And sometimes it includes chancing rejection, disapproval, or ridicule by telling someone that you are attracted to him or her, turning down the invitation to your family's annual reunion or pitching an innovative idea to your coworkers.

The vast majority of us view openness as risky at best and often out of the question entirely. Indeed, many of us employ open agendas *only* as a last resort or when:

- relatively little is at stake;
- the person involved is either someone who has earned our trust or is perceived as nonthreatening;
- we have little or no emotional investment in the issue being discussed or the outcome of the situation.

The "Are They *Really* Being Open?" Checklist

Anything that you or other people actually say or do is technically out in the open. You can see it, hear it, or otherwise use your basic senses to observe it. However, those words and actions may reveal just the tip of the iceberg and conceal or misrepresent what is really going on below the surface or they can be a true representation of actual and acknowledged thoughts and feelings—in other words, an open agenda. How do you tell the difference? To help you figure that out, here is a checklist of clues to look for during any interaction.

_____ Is the message clear? Regardless of any hemming and hawing, stuttering and rephrasing brought on by the all-too-common resistance to honest self-expression, does what is being conveyed seem to make sense?

_____ Is the message complete? Is this person explaining himself fully and voluntarily providing details that help you understand his point of view?

———— If you ask questions, are they answered willingly and directly?

———— Are words, body language, facial expressions, tone of voice, and other nonverbal signals in alignment—consistent with each other and conveying the same message? [Someone using an open agenda will *not* say, "I guess you know what you're doing" in a tone of voice that conveys skepticism, as Jane did. They will *not* claim that nothing is wrong while stomping around the kitchen, as Kate did.]

———— Does the emotional intensity of the message fit the circumstances? [Neither an overreaction like Sara's response to her mother nor an attempt to show no reaction like Barry's approach to Eddie.]

———— Are the points being made open to discussion?

———— Do you feel comfortable with the interaction; virtually free of anxiety or insecurity; and connected to, rather than alienated from, the person with whom you are interacting?

If all eight questions receive "yes" answers, in all probability you have encountered an open agenda. If you come up with one or more "no" answers, then something may be going on below the surface. However, if all but the last question receive "yes" answers, I advise you *not* to jump to the conclusion that the person with whom you are interacting is hiding something from you. Although this may indeed be the case, there are several other possibilities to consider first.

Amanda, who is in her mid-thirties, single, and generally ambivalent about men and relationships, told me about a conversation with a man, several years younger than she, whom she had just begun dating.

"At the end of our second date," she recalled, "he sat me down and said, 'I'm really attracted to you and I want to spend more time with you, but I have to do this two-week training thing for the army reserves and I'm pretty worked up about it. You'll probably think I'm nuts, but there's a lot of physical activity involved and I'm not in the greatest shape. I'm scared I'll have a heart attack or something. So I just want to put things on hold until I get back. But I will call you as soon as I do."

A survivor of countless encounters with men who seemed interested, said they would call and then did not, Amanda's immediate inclination was to write off her date as just another in a long line of what she calls "jerks in nice-guy clothing." Indeed, she decided that what appeared to be a heartfelt revelation was "just a better-than-average con job." Assuming that she would never again hear from the young man, she spent two weeks feeling disappointed and disillusioned because she had been very drawn to him and had high hopes that a solid, lasting relationship could develop.

As it turned out, the fortnight of misery was completely unnecessary. Amanda did not recognize it, but what she had seen and heard had been what was really going on and all that was going on. Her date had been honest with her, called as he said he would and at last report, the couple was looking for an apartment to share.

Because of the skepticism left over from her past experiences, Amanda dismissed all the clues indicating that her date was using an open agenda. "Looking back on it now," Amanda explained, "I realize that what I was skeptical about was the fact that he had been so open with me in the first place"—which was a reflection of the assumptions in her agenda, not his.

Because interactions involving open agendas may be the exception rather than the rule in your life, when you encounter someone who is using one, you, too, may be taken aback. In fact, like Amanda, you may feel every bit as anxious and bewildered as you would if hidden motives *were* present.

Or you may be reacting to the fact that even though

what is happening is open and aboveboard, you still do not like it. After all, openness is not synonymous with agreement or satisfaction and conflicts occur even when you and others are fully aware of your own needs and make them clear to each other. What's more, if you are concealing or camouflaging your real motives, someone else's open agenda, no matter how purely motivated, can backfire—as Michael's certainly did. He recognized his own need to get off the phone and meet with his boss. He clearly conveyed that to Kate. Unfortunately, because she was experiencing needs and emotions which she had chosen not to reveal to Michael, but hoped that he would recognize anyway, Kate was hurt and put off by Michael's openness. In fact, she took it as a sign that he did not care about her feelings. This was not Michael's intention, of course, but it was what happened— and is hardly an uncommon occurrence.

Hidden Agendas

Whenever you recognize your own needs, fears, and wishes but choose to conceal, camouflage or misrepresent them— rather than make them known to other people—you have *a hidden agenda.*

Hidden agendas are based on the assumption that things are more likely to work out the way we want them to if we hide what we want in the first place. On paper, this premise may seem absurd. However, as you no doubt realized while reading the last chapter, in real life that is precisely how we operate.

If we could read between the lines of Jane and Sara's interaction over the dinner preparation, it might go something like this:

As soon as Sara put a casserole into the oven, Jane casually walked over to it and glanced at the temperature dial.

[Jane: *I'm positive she has this set too high. If I tell her, she'll think I'm interfering. If I don't tell her, the casserole will burn. I don't want to start an argument, but I do know that I'm right. Maybe, if I just ask her nicely . . .*]

"Don't you have this set too high?" Jane asked.

[Sara: *There she goes, butting in again. If I had a nickel for every time this week that she's had some know-it-all comment about the way I do things, I'd be an independently wealthy woman. I'm really furious, but if I show that, we'll both end up yelling. So, I'll just take a deep breath and . . .*]

"No, Mother," Sara replied. "I've made that casserole dozens of times and I always use that setting."

[Jane: *And I'll bet she always overcooks the casserole, too. She is so stubborn, always turning down perfectly good advice. I want her to know that she doesn't know everything. But I want her to get that message without looking like a buttinsky or picking a fight . . .*]

"Well, I guess you know what you're doing," Jane said in a tone of voice indicating that she thought quite the opposite.

At this point, Sara could no longer keep her true feelings hidden. The anger she had buried throughout her mother's visit and no doubt throughout any number of previous visits exploded to the surface.

Interactions that involve hidden agendas tend to irritate and infuriate as well as baffle those of us on the receiving end of them. However, when we are the ones using them, those agendas not only make perfect sense to us, but also seem completely justifiable. We can always come up with a viable reason for choosing an indirect rather than a direct approach.

Practicing the Art of Deception

Psychiatrist and author R. D. Laing once said, "I have never come across a family that does not draw a line somewhere as to what may be put into words and what words it may be put into." From our families and in many other settings as well, we absorbed the rules and norms governing what is appropriate to reveal and what is best kept a secret. These social constraints are one of the reasons that most of us simply do not share our innermost thoughts or feelings (and in certain situations, not even our surface ones). Witness the waiter who politely recites the daily specials even though what he'd really like to say is, "You idiot, they're listed on the card clipped to your menu." Observe the employee who yesses her boss while fully intending to do things her own way, or the couple who tell each other they had a wonderful evening (when they really couldn't wait for the evening to end). Lies lubricate social life. And being tactful, which is after all a valued trait, prevents us from challenging these socially acceptable deceits.

The secrets we keep from others and the camouflage we use to disguise our true intentions may be as innocuous and easy to read as hiding a self-disclosure in a general statement of opinion. "I've always thought men with dark hair and blue eyes were particularly attractive," the young woman says to a young man with dark hair and blue eyes, and you do not need any special skills to figure out what she means—she is attracted to him. Hidden agendas can be dangerous, as attempting to probe your lover's feelings about you by stirring up jealousy—a potentially explosive hidden agenda if ever there was one; or they can be frustrating, as the extremely common "If you cared, you would know how I'm feeling" test that Kate administered. When using this hidden agenda, you keep certain needs or feelings hidden and hope that your partner will guess what they are. If he or she doesn't do this immediately, you provide a few clues. You pout or sigh, become quieter than usual, or storm about slamming doors and stomping your feet. If your partner still doesn't get the message, you make your signals more obvious, but you still don't reveal what's actually going on. If he loved me, you think, then he would know. Similar tests are administered at work, with our family and friends and in therapy.

In addition to the defensive maneuvers, power plays, and self-deceptions I included in the previous chapter, other readily recognizable forms of deception include:

- the paranoid shield—taking on a threatening demeanor to scare off your "enemies," as Eddie did, going on the offensive to defend yourself before someone else gets a chance to trigger your insecurities and fears;
- backing off and clamming up—in personal relationships, distancing yourself from others so they will pursue you, try to get closer and let you know that they care; in business, saying nothing so that the other person begins to squirm, reveals information that you need, or acquiesces to your point of view.
- the double bind—sending two contradictory messages, usually one verbally and the other nonverbally. Thrown two information balls—one stamped in invisible ink—the other person receives both messages but does not know which one to respond to. You are able to protect yourself from an unwanted reaction because you can either deny that you sent the covert message or insist that she should have "read between the lines" of the up-front communication.

Hidden agendas can also be disguised as open ones, which is often what happens when the man you meet at a singles event plays the part of a sensitive guy in order to

entice you into his bed or when your boss takes on the role of
a concerned parent figure so that she can weasel information
out of you.

Are *You* Being Deceived?
The Hidden Agenda Checklist

Although hidden agendas are difficult to understand and respond to, they are easy to spot. Most of the time we can sense
when what we see is *not* the whole picture. However, unless
we catch someone in an outright lie, we are apt to dismiss
such suspicions from our minds. To confirm that something is
going on below the surface and make conscious choices about
how to proceed, we need a bit more evidence than our gut
instincts offer us. Here are some questions you can ask yourself during or after encounters that seem to have more going
on than meets the eye. These signs may indicate that a hidden
agenda is operating.

_____ Are there inconsistencies between what this person
is saying and how he is saying it, or other actions
that do not fit the immediate circumstances? [Is your
boss glaring at you angrily while telling you he did
not mind that while he was out of the office you
went to his boss with a problem? Does a client as-
sure you that he is hanging on your every word—
even though he keeps looking around the restaurant
as you speak or keeps directing his gaze at your
cleavage? Is your friend sneaking some barbed comments in between her smiles and laughter?]

_____ Does what you hear or witness in the present situation contradict something you have been told or led
to believe in the past?

_____ Is crucial information omitted? [For example, does a

coworker, who wants you to side with her against your boss, go into great detail about the unfair treatment she just received, while neglecting to mention that she had been late eight times in a month and was caught asleep at her desk prior to the confrontation she is describing?]

———— Is this person beating around the bush instead of making the point? Is the interaction riddled with innuendo and strategic ambiguity? [Watch out for phrases like "Get my drift?", "Obviously, I don't have to explain this to you," or "I'm sure you know what I mean," which are clear indications that this person either assumes that you already know something that he is not telling you or expects you to guess about what he really means.]

———— Does the person to whom you are speaking seem minimally attentive at best? Does he or she say, "Uh huh," "Really," or "I see," at appropriate intervals but seem impatient, distracted, or a million miles away? Chances are that the other person is letting you say your piece but has no intention of taking it seriously or changing his or her opinion on the matter at hand.

———— Is the "repeater effect" operating? Regardless of what you say, does the other person make essentially the same points he has already made several times before? [This is usually a sign that the other person has already made a decision that she is not revealing to you or is covering up a mistake or protecting a "sore spot" that she does not want you to know about.]

———— Are you anxious? Is your stomach knotting, your heart pounding, or palms sweating? Can you hear that little voice in the back of your mind asking, "What's really going on here?"

If your answer to one or more of these questions is "yes," chances are that you are not "just being paranoid," but have indeed encountered a hidden agenda.

When Hidden Agendas Backfire

There is no doubt that the major benefit of using hidden agendas is that they often work for us. At one time or another, the indirect route has indeed gotten us to the goal line and enabled us to get our own way.

Unfortunately, we have a tendency to use this indirect approach indiscriminately—whenever we feel the slightest twinge of anxiety or can convince ourselves that revealing what is really on our minds would cause some sort of unpleasantness we'd prefer not to hassle with. However, as you discovered while completing the secret-keeping self-test, using hidden agendas in situations that warrant them can cause countless problems.

I witnessed one such problem firsthand while working as a consultant to a social service agency. It was public knowledge that, because of a shortfall in the state budget, funding to the agency would be cut. There were many ways that the agency could have handled the cutbacks, but the director quickly decided that he would institute a hiring freeze as of January 1, so that existing vacancies and new ones caused by attrition would not be filled. Believing that the news of his decision would destroy the morale of his already overworked and underpaid staff, the director chose not to tell them about it. Instead, he told them that he had not made a decision yet. Rumors spread through the agency like wildfire and employees spent a good portion of the workday worrying and speculating about layoffs, pay cuts, and elimination of important programs—all worse than what the director had decided to do. Morale plummeted and the angry, frightened staff was on the verge of becoming an unruly mob.

As you can see, the director's hidden agenda approach, which he thought would prevent lowered morale, ended up creating it. And any hidden agenda has the potential to turn on you that way or even blow up in your face the way it did for Kate and Michael, who took their first steps in the direction of disaster when Michael, short on time and with other things on his mind, missed his cues and therefore did not do what Kate expected or needed him to do. The fact that she had not exactly broadcast her needs did not completely escape Kate, of course. "I had a feeling Michael didn't realize that he'd hurt me by hanging up so quickly," she admitted. "But I also felt like he should have known that it would upset me." And so she set out to make sure he got that message. But once he did, Michael got angry and vengefully decided to "give Kate a dose of her own medicine." When the couple arrived at my office for their weekly therapy session, they were barely speaking to each other, and both were completely miserable. Kate's original needs remained unfulfilled and new problems had been generated. Her hidden agenda had backfired, leaving a trail of conflict, mistrust, and hurt feelings in its wake.

OPEN OR HIDDEN: WHICH WILL YOU CHOOSE?

When everyone involved in an interaction operates with open agendas, all parties are more likely to get at least some of their needs met. Even when you and others do not see eye to eye, open agendas make negotiation and compromise possible. Of course, you are bound to encounter situations in which you are using an open agenda while other people are oblivious to their own agendas or consciously keeping parts of them hidden. Even so, you can still derive satisfaction from the fact that you are being true to yourself. If you continue to use an open agenda even in the face of other people's hidden or automatic ones, you increase your chances of being heard and understood as well as resolving problems constructively. What's more, openness feels good, providing those "in the moment" moments when you can sense that you are truly connecting and effectively communicating with others.

In spite of these benefits, complete honesty is not always the best policy. In fact, open agendas work in your best interest only when you use them judiciously and *not* when:

- your revelation will hurt someone else;
- the truth is intended to hurt someone else, becoming more ammunition in the ongoing psychological warfare between yourself and another person;
- there is a reasonable possibility that another person will use the information against you, reveal it to others without your permission, or add it to the list of vulnerabilities he can exploit at a later date;
- you automatically assume that, because you are being open and aboveboard, the person with whom you are interacting is too.

As I said in the Introduction, this book is about making conscious choices that are in your best interest—and that is not what you are doing if you assume that a completely uncensored open agenda is the answer to every problem. As you learn more about yourself and others, you may, in fact, consciously choose to be more open more often. However, you should not expect to "let it all hang out," "tell it like it is," or "lay your cards on the table" in all situations with all people. There is—to quote systems theorist Gregory Bateson —"always an optimal value beyond which anything is toxic, no matter what: oxygen, sleep, psychotherapy, philosophy . . ." and honesty.

Of course, most of us have a way to go before we need

to worry about overdosing on honesty. In fact, we may be in danger of drowning in a sea of secrecy because it seems as if every situation we encounter calls for a defensive maneuver, power play, or self-deception. We conceal, camouflage, and misrepresent our real motives without even considering the consequences of our other options. Indeed, we may not even know we have a hidden agenda or what we are actually hiding. We are unwittingly keeping secrets from ourselves as well as others because we are under the influence of the third kind of agenda—an *automatic* one.

Automatic Agendas

When the counseling services coordinator position, which Barry was ultimately chosen to fill, became available, Eddie assumed that it would be offered to him. Tired and fed up with working on the alcohol detoxification unit, Eddie saw the promotion as his way out of an unsatisfying work situation. What's more, he believed that the administration of the rehabilitation hospital owed him something for his years of service and fully expected them to pay up by promoting him. Instead, they hired Barry, who was younger and had less counseling experience than he. Eddie, as you might expect, was outraged.

"I paid my dues," he grumbled. "Gave seven years to this place and ten more in other programs. My experience should have counted for more than Barry's fancy degrees and fancy management theories."

According to Eddie, the administration had added insult to injury when they decided not to hire someone from within the ranks. "An outsider can't understand what it's really like to work here," he insisted. An early mistake Barry made during his first few weeks of adjusting to his new job seemed to prove Eddie's point. Not only had he been passed up for a promotion he believed he deserved, but he was being supervised by an "idiot."

Perhaps you could guess that those items were on Eddie's psychological agenda and it is worth noting that several other counselors shared Eddie's feelings and were initially as hostile and argumentative as he. However, Barry, who was in fact a skilled and insightful supervisor, anticipated that reaction and made a conscious effort to show his respect for his staff's expertise and experience, to include them in decision-making, to get to know them as unique individuals and help them resolve any problems they brought to him. Yet Eddie continued to perceive everything Barry did as unjust or abusive—even when it was not. He made unreasonable demands —like wanting to be called to regularly scheduled staff meetings—and when they were not met, he used it as proof that he was being mistreated and felt that his anger and hostility were more justified than ever.

Eddie felt tense and furious throughout each workday. His friends and colleagues repeatedly pointed out that his belligerent behavior could cost him his job and was already aggravating everyone around him. Eddie even made resolutions to lighten up and not let Barry bother him so much. "But I just couldn't stop myself," he said. And indeed he could not. Eddie's attitudes and actions were automatic. They met a need that Eddie *did not even know he had,* enabling him to protect himself from more disturbing ideas—in this instance, the fact that he did *not* really deserve a promotion, that he was not qualified to be a supervisor, had made no effort to increase his skills or knowledge and had spent most of those seven years on the job doing just enough to get by and no more. As long as Eddie's attention was focused on how stupid, incompetent, overrated, and insensitive Barry was, Eddie did not have to face those facts. He did not have to look inward at his own less-than-optimal attributes and risk thinking less of himself. He did not know he was doing this. His desire not to face the unpleasant facts about himself was *unconscious*. The tactics he could not help himself from using were deeply ingrained *habits*. And his motives and methods were items on his *automatic agenda*.

Automatic agendas, like open or hidden ones, contain certain needs, wishes, and expectations that you try to fulfill. However, the items on your automatic agenda *are as much a mystery to* you *as they are to other people*. You truly do not recognize them and therefore can neither understand them nor effectively control their impact on your thoughts, feelings, and actions. What you do while under the influence of an automatic agenda is not a choice, but a habit. You do not intentionally lie, conceal, or deceive as you do when you have a hidden agenda. You *unintentionally* distort and deny, so that what you present to others is the absolute truth—as you see it. Of course, it isn't the whole truth, nor is it reality as someone else would see it, because your automatic agenda compels you to keep secrets from yourself.

All automatic agendas contain at least one vital link to your past experiences—even though you may not see the connection immediately or consider it significant. They are most likely to kick in and take over when you experience circumstances that resemble unsettling or upsetting situations you have encountered before—*even if you do not recognize the resemblance.* Eleven months after her first ill-fated in-service training session, Jenny was more bothered by her bewildering behavior than ever. And she had good reason to be. She found herself altering her presentation after even the slightest sign of disinterest. Every yawn, twitch, and fidget derailed her train of thought.

Jenny's behavior baffled her audience. It baffled her as well. Indeed, she did not even recognize what she was doing until after she began to do it, and by then her mind was racing like a runaway train.

"I don't know what's going on," Jenny sighed. "I really don't." Yet something quite similar had gone on throughout Jenny's childhood, when she would try to outsmart and entertain her alcoholic father in hopes of preventing his drinking binges or his explosiveness when he was already drunk. "I was very young, maybe four or five, when I noticed that there were things I did, especially when my dad had been drinking, that made him smile or laugh," Jenny recalled. "And somehow, that sort of became my job, to keep Daddy happy so that he wouldn't yell or throw things or hit us. I did keep a pretty close eye on him, because he could go off in an instant. I had a whole list of things that he enjoyed, little songs I'd sing or imitations of TV characters that I'd do or animal faces. Sometimes I had to run through my whole repertoire."

As Jenny got older, her "job description" expanded. She, like several other members of her family and many children of alcoholics, decided that if she tried hard enough, she could keep her father from drinking. Again she took note of any little nuance of his behavior that signaled an impending binge and, in hopes of "cutting him off at the pass," tried everything from hiding liquor bottles to feigning injuries just as he was heading out the door. "Once I staged a fall down the steps and actually wound up breaking my arm," she sighed. "My ploys had maybe a 35 percent success rate, but when they succeeded I felt like I was the smartest kid in the world. And when they didn't, I felt I was the dumbest, especially when he got really angry about what I tried to do. I remember times when I'd be standing at the door, watching him drive away and thinking 'I'm so stupid, stupid, stupid.' I hated that feeling." Jenny still does, so much so that she unwittingly goes to almost any length to avoid feeling that way —which was precisely what she did during her in-service seminars.

You see, as a result of her childhood experiences, Jenny

came to believe that she had to please other people or something terrible would happen and that being smart was absolutely essential to her safety and survival. Etched into the recesses of her mind, these expectations of herself and the signs that she might not be living up to them became part of her automatic agenda. So did the methods she used to meet her own standards—automatically responding to signs of disinterest or displeasure by pulling some new attention-grabber from her ever-growing bag of tricks. Even though she did not recognize the similarities, the in-service sessions replicated certain elements of her earlier experiences. Members of her audience who appeared to be smarter than she or who seemed bored with her presentation posed a threat that she had encountered in the past, and even though she was not aware of feeling threatened, Jenny automatically tried to protect herself. Driven by invisible forces, she tried to "cut them off at the pass" as she had so often done during her interactions with her father. Unfortunately, she ended up getting off the track and losing control of the situation instead.

Automatic agendas are also activated by emotions that may never get close enough to the surface for you to realize you are feeling them. *They are behind almost any thought, feeling, or behavior that we label irrational, incomprehensible, or uncontrollable.*

Fitting this description to a tee, Eddie's attitudes and actions were motivated by cold, raw fear. Born poor, growing up on the streets and quitting school "as soon as I could do it without getting picked up for truancy," Eddie abused drugs and ran with a gang. "It's a miracle I lived to see my eighteenth birthday," he claims. After his brother got knifed in a gang fight and his best friend died from a drug overdose, Eddie, thinking that he, too, was heading for an early grave, obtained his high school equivalency degree, joined the army, and eventually graduated from college with a degree in substance abuse counseling. He had gotten his act together, but the fact of the matter was that together or not, in Eddie's mind it was still an act. Buried deep in Eddie's unconscious was an image of himself as inherently inadequate and the belief that he had only escaped poverty and despair by sheer luck—which could change for the worse at any minute.

Eddie was scared to death, but he did not know it because any thought that was too painful and terrifying to acknowledge got turned around before Eddie became consciously aware of it. Eddie never felt afraid because he never saw the actions and attitudes he feared could lead to his demise in himself, but only in other people. Thus, from Eddie's perspective—distorted by his automatic agenda—Barry was the one who was inadequate and got his job because of a lucky break. Barry's unfair treatment—not Eddie's blatant disregard for hospital policies—was going to "ruin everything" for Eddie. Eddie even got to fight off his fears by fighting with Barry.

Automatic agendas are the driving force behind the repetitive patterns in our lives, compelling us to engage in the same behaviors over and over again—even though our own habits are making us miserable. They are:

- the defensive maneuvers, power plays, and self-deceptions you use without thinking and continue to use even though they are not working;
- the promises you make—to quit drinking, to quit fighting with your spouse about money, to find more time to relax or spend less time alone watching TV— and then break;
- attracting the same kind of lovers or friends, feeling as stifled by your present job as you felt about every other job you've ever had, or asking yourself, "How did I get myself into the same old mess again?"

These behaviors can all be blamed on your automatic agenda. Somewhere along the line you developed a habit of acting or reacting in a certain way. You didn't know you were doing it, and now that you are aware of the unpleasant results of it you may wish you could break the habit, but it isn't easy. "I just can't help myself," you say. "I want to stop, but I just can't."

Are You Acting Under the Influence of an Automatic Agenda? The Checklist

Perhaps you are thinking—with a certain amount of relief— that you don't go to the extremes that Eddie and Jenny do, that you are not so out of control. In fact, based on what you've read so far, you may be saying to yourself, "I always know what I'm doing. So I guess I must be one of those people who doesn't have an automatic agenda."

All of us have automatic agendas, but most of us do not think that we do. The fact that we sometimes act irrationally, the idea that we might not be in control at all times, and the possibility that something we do not know about may be buried somewhere in the depths of our minds are also secrets that we keep from ourselves. Even so, you can at times glimpse your own automatic agenda in action.

For instance, you may have a sense of being out of sync, of doing something other than what you set out to—as Sara did when she consciously decided to keep her cool with her mother but exploded anyway. If you bungle a task you have done many times before, forget something you would normally remember, experience slips of the tongue, or miss the freeway exit that you use on your way to or from work every day—chances are that you are fulfilling a wish that you have not acknowledged to yourself.

And as was the case with hidden agendas, your feelings can also tip you off to the presence of concealed material.

Extreme, disproportionate, and highly emotional reactions to certain people or situations often indicate that you are responding to something more than what is really going on at that moment—something contained in your automatic agendas.

Here are some other clues you can pick up from your own behavior (and other people's, if you suspect that an automatic agenda is making them unreasonable or difficult to deal with).

_____ Losing your train of thought and/or suddenly falling silent.

_____ Forgetting what you wanted to or meant to say (for example, leaving out the most important task on the list of chores you are discussing with your child-care worker; or when someone you had tried to reach earlier returns your call, drawing a complete blank about what you had wanted to discuss with that person).

_____ Changes in your speech patterns—stuttering, lisping, losing your voice, talking louder or more rapidly than usual, repeating yourself and so on.

_____ Reactions that do not fit the circumstances you have encountered, including *overreactions* (pitching a fit because you missed a bus, even though another will pull up in five minutes and still get you to your appointment with time to spare); *little or no reaction* (having someone blow up at you—and then immediately and calmly going back to whatever you were doing before the disruption); or *odd reactions* (laughing when something frightening—like learning that your son has been taken to the emergency room—happens, or marching up to someone fully intending to assert yourself and express your anger, but starting to cry as soon as you open your mouth to speak).

_____ Rushes of emotion out of the blue—feeling anxious, sad, giddy, angry, or afraid and being unable to pinpoint any immediate circumstance that might be prompting you to feel that way.

_____ Physical symptoms like ulcers, bad backs, headaches, asthma, or upset stomachs which act up periodically (usually when you are upset but do not know it).

_____ Unbidden and unstoppable thoughts (like Beverly's visions of her husband's death or simply reviewing over and over again everything that happened on a date which might have turned off the other person).

_____ Repeated actions that you are unable to discontinue through willpower alone (constant hand washing, list making, binge eating, workaholism, checking an alarm clock every five minutes to see if it is set, and any other compulsive behavior).

_____ Hearing comments—on more than a few occasions from more than a few people—about your behavior that you think are "off the wall" or completely unfounded.

This last clue warrants closer examination, since one frequent aspect of automatic agendas is that other people can spot our self-defeating habits and repetitive behavior patterns far more easily than we can. This should come as no surprise. After all, you have no doubt experienced the phenomenon in reverse—finding other people's automatic behavior so irritatingly obvious that you are amazed that they do not recognize it themselves. Indeed, at least part of your frustration with the bewildering people in your life stems from the fact that they not only do the same dumb things over and over again, but also insist that they do not do those things at all.

When you are the person who sees the patterns in someone else's behavior and finds the reasons behind the actions to be quite transparent, you practically want to shake that person for not seeing what is so transparent to you. However, when someone else points out your patterns to you, you, too, are shocked and unwilling or unable to see the light. Under these circumstances, neither you nor other people are being stupid or stubborn. You see, every automatic agenda comes with a complementary set of blinders that prevent you from recognizing certain details of what you do while acting under the influence of your automatic agenda.

But are we really keeping these things secret from ourselves? you may wonder. If we really concentrated, couldn't we recognize our underlying motives and understand why we do what we do, think what we think, and feel what we feel?

The answer to both questions is yes. Yes, you can really keep secrets from yourself, and you do whenever one part of your mind (the unconscious) knows what it is doing while the part that is supposed to know (the conscious) remains oblivious. That is what happens when you operate on auto-pilot and will be discussed again in Chapter 7. However, there are also countless thoughts and feelings that lie just below the surface. You could dig them up and use them to your advantage if you just paid more attention to what you were remembering and telling yourself about yourself.

4

What's on Your Agenda?

How to Stop, Look, and Listen to Your Characteristic Responses

Greg is a special education teacher who once viewed himself —and was perceived by others—as a concerned, creative, energetic, and dedicated educator. "I used to be really involved with my students and their families," he explained. "I was up on all the latest teaching methods and couldn't wait to use them in my classroom. Most of the time I wound up with the kids everyone else thought of as hopeless cases. But all they needed was that little bit extra that I don't seem to have anymore." Indeed, according to Greg, he no longer has enough energy or interest to do even the bare minimum required of him.

"It's all I can do to get out of bed in the morning," he claimed. "I use the same old lesson plans. Hell, I haven't

even changed my bulletin boards in the last three months.
I'm short-tempered with the kids and I complain constantly.
I've turned into exactly the kind of teacher I used to hate."

What caused this dramatic turnaround? Although a variety of factors played a part in undermining his efficiency and
enthusiasm, Greg, as he put it, "really began to go downhill"
when a new principal was assigned to his school.

"The old principal was very supportive and understanding," he said. "She was a big believer in positive reinforce-
ment. When you did well she was right there patting you on
the back, which made me want to do even better."

Grace, the new principal, was the exact opposite. She
viewed her position as primarily administrative and appeared
to be more interested in paperwork than people. "Grace has
a hands-off policy," Greg sighed. "She pays absolutely no
attention to her teachers unless they do something wrong and
then she comes down on them with a vengeance. I've never
heard her say anything nice to anybody. Not one encouraging word has ever escaped her lips."

Although he immediately missed his former principal's
support and recognition, Greg at first gave Grace the benefit
of the doubt. But when four months passed without any positive feedback from Grace, he decided to take action—indi-
rectly. He used a setup to get some recognition and encouragement from Grace. "My class was completing a unit on
space travel and they had done some really exciting things,"
he recalled. "So I invited her to be there for the last lesson,
which was just incredible and went off without a hitch." Unfortunately, Grace did not take the bait. "She stayed all of
five minutes," he grumbled, "and never gave me one word
of feedback. Nothing. You would have thought that my class
and I and the whole thing was completely invisible to her."

Over the next few months, Greg tried time and again to
get Grace to show some appreciation for the work he was

doing. "I was working harder than I ever had and though I got satisfaction from watching my students learn and grow, I got absolutely no recognition for my efforts from Grace," he complained. What's more, Greg was not the only one who was fed up, and whenever two or more teachers gathered, a gripe session began. "Everyone was furious and frustrated," Greg continued. "Morale was at an all-time low." Slowly but steadily, Greg began to devote less time and energy to his job and derived less satisfaction from it. "You can just give so much when you are not getting enough back," he sighed. "I gave as much as I could and then I just gave up."

Greg wanted, expected, and indeed *needed* a certain amount of recognition, encouragement, and appreciation from his boss as well as his students in order to feel good about himself, confirm his competence as a teacher, and maintain the energy and enthusiasm his demanding job required. When he was getting what he needed from his old principal, Greg was able to perform efficiently and effectively. He was like a fully fueled automobile after a tune-up —capable of getting wherever it had to go. Regrettably, like a car that is not maintained properly, when Greg's needs stopped being met—because Grace withheld the additional support he required—Greg was unable to function as he had in the past. He began to falter and feel as if "everything was out of whack"—which is how most of us feel when a specific situation or ongoing relationship is not in sync with our psychological agendas. This is, of course, most likely to occur when one or more people involved in an interaction or relationship have hidden agendas.

You see, although you may not recognize or understand what is happening when more is going on than meets the eye, you will at some level recognize what is *not* happening—that the needs, hopes, and desires in your agenda are not being fulfilled, that you:

- feel unappreciated or ignored by people whose approval you desire;
- have been forced by organizational or other changes to give up something you were accustomed to;
- have encountered people who withhold the information or guidance you require to function comfortably and effectively;
- will not be getting what you want or expect to get at work, in your marriage or relationship, from your parents, children, friends, or even from yourself.

When this occurs, you may not actually say "This situation is frustrating the hell out of me," or "This relationship is not meeting my needs." In fact, you may be aware of no more than a sinking feeling in the pit of your stomach or you may squelch distressing emotions so quickly that you never consciously recognize those feelings at all. However, your unmet needs *always* register in some corner of your mind, creating an internal imbalance, a sense that you are being deprived of something that seems vital to you. And you invariably feel compelled to do *something* to restore your sense of equilibrium.

At that point, do you carefully analyze your immediate circumstances or consider the various alternatives available to you? Probably not. When faced with baffling, nerve-wracking circumstances, the vast majority of us go directly from stimulus to response—automatically employing a limited number of methods we typically use to get our own way. That approach is often one that worked for us in the past and that we have had ample opportunity to practice over the years. Indeed, you may have practiced it so much that it is now a habit and your *characteristic* response to many different circumstances.

How to Spot a Characteristic Response

Characteristic responses to baffling and frustrating situations
include any of the defensive maneuvers, power plays, or self-
deceptions I've previously mentioned (see Chapter 2), pitching a fit, getting depressed, physically escaping from the situation by walking out of the house or away from the person
who is irritating you, fleeing psychologically with the help of
distracting activities or mood-altering substances like alcohol
or caffeine, or ruminating about the problem. They can also
be generally positive and useful coping strategies like expressing your feelings, clearing the air by talking about what
is happening, looking for solutions to the problems you have
encountered, asking questions to confirm or clarify the message you seem to be receiving and so on. It is not what you
say or do that makes your response a characteristic one, but
rather that you respond in that manner *indiscriminately.* Instead of tailoring or tempering your reaction to fit the immediate circumstances, you pursue a course of action simply
because it is familiar and comfortable. How can you tell if
this is what you are doing? You can start by learning to spot a
characteristic response when you see one. Here are some
telltale signs:

- You have attempted to solve problems or get your
  own way in this manner on numerous occasions in the
  past—and you can recall times when this particular approach did indeed work for you.
- You react this way in a variety of settings and situations (at home, at work, while caught in a traffic jam,
  with your children, your parents, your boss, a sales
  clerk who overcharges you, a receptionist who puts
  you on hold for five minutes).
- It is generally the first and often the only coping strategy that you employ.

- It may be the first suggestion that comes to mind when other people ask you to advise them on what to do about their problems.

- Although you can in retrospect rationalize the course of action you pursued, before you took action you did not have a specific or particularly logical reason for what you did or said.

- Other people act as if your actions are completely predictable, making comments like, "You're always doing that," or "There you go again," or "I wish I had a dime for every time you told me that." They may even interrupt the story you are relating to say, "Don't tell me. You . . ." and then describe your behavior to a tee.

When your response does not have the desired effect, you are shocked and dismayed. You are unable to view the situation as objectively as you would if you had considered other alternatives and their possible repercussions ahead of time or tailored your response to fit the immediate circumstances. You cannot say, "I did what I thought was best," or "Okay, plan A didn't work. Let's try plan B." Instead, you are apt to rail against the other person in the interaction or berate yourself unmercifully and feel more anxious and powerless than ever.

Again, there may be nothing inherently wrong with your characteristic response. When it is appropriate to the situation in which you are using it, your typical approach can certainly be in your best interest.

More often than not, however, we use our comfortable and familiar responses even though these no longer fit the situation—which is about as practical as buying clothing in the size you've always worn even though you have lost or gained thirty pounds. What's more, although we may be aware of what we are doing, at no time do we say "Gee, I'm

the past to distort his thinking in the present, convincing him that using a hidden agenda was in his best interest, when in fact it was not.

The thoughts and feelings associated with incomplete, usually unpleasant past experiences rise to the top of your psychological agenda whenever you encounter people or events that remind you of those old experiences. Your memories cloud your judgment, frequently convincing you that your present-day circumstances are more dangerous or hopeless than they really are.

In Mark's case he reacted to someone who had actually been a source of distress in the recent and distant past. You may do this, too, acting like a rebellious adolescent in the presence of your parents or getting tongue-tied and feeling guilty when you run into the Sunday school teacher who taught you right from wrong. However, you also act out old scenes in new settings with new actors in the starring roles. In fact, a good many of the baffling situations you encounter remind you of something that happened in the past. The cue can be almost anything.

- Learning that your lover is leaving on a three-day business trip, you suddenly cannot stop thinking about a former lover. On closer inspection, you remember that he came home from a business trip and announced that your relationship was over.
- The tone of voice your boss uses when he is being friendly and playfully teasing you makes you anxious, but you don't know why until you realize it is the same tone of voice a teacher used when he humiliated you during gym class.
- You prepare yourself for disappointment and give up without really trying whenever you are called upon to compete with coworkers for a promotion. In the back of your mind the ancient memory of how you felt each

time your parents paid more attention to your brother than to you keeps you from getting ahead.

Whatever it is, the connection between past and present convinces you that you will be more likely to get what you want and less likely to suffer unpleasant consequences if you use a hidden agenda.

Since you usually do not know that you are remembering, much less *what* you are remembering, you naturally assume that your interpretation of the events going on around you is accurate (even though it may not even be in the ballpark) and that your reactions are appropriate and justified by the immediate circumstances (even though they do not work and are out of proportion to the situation). This, as you have seen, is a prescription for disaster. Fortunately, it is a prescription that you can rewrite. The next chapter—on old agendas—will provide valuable insights for actually completing and letting go of your unfinished business. But you do not have to accomplish that feat in order to keep old messages from getting in your way. You can start now to find out which messages are on your agenda.

What Are You Remembering?

The next time you encounter a situation in which you could use a hidden agenda or an open one, a drastic maneuver or a subtle one, stop and ask yourself what unfinished business may have risen to the top of your agenda. Here are some questions you can use to uncover what you are remembering in specific situations, or to unravel any mysterious ongoing interactions you have been having with your spouse or lover, boss or coworkers, friends, or neighbors. Although they are most helpful when posed *before* you take action, until you get into the habit of doing that, you can learn a great deal by exploring them after the fact.

Please note that you do not need to go all the way back to your childhood in order to answer these questions. Recalling more recent events can also reveal useful information.

RECALL EXERCISE 2

What does this situation remind me of?

What usually happens to me in situations like this one?

How do I usually react to what usually happens?

Is what happened then what is *really* happening now? What else could be happening?

RECALL EXERCISE 3

Who does this person remind me of?

How did I feel about that person?

How did I (or do I) typically behave in that person's presence?

How is this person *different* from the person he reminds me of?

How am I *different* than I was when I interacted with that other person?

RECALL EXERCISE 4

How am I feeling right now?

When have I felt this way before?

What did I do on the previous occasions that I felt this way?

Why did I do what I did then? Was I in a defenseless position then? Did I have fewer coping skills, less knowledge, limited emotional support?

What do I have now that I did not have then?

Why *don't* I have to feel this way or feel this strongly now?

Self-concept

Do any of these statements sound familiar?

- "I have the reverse Midas touch. Instead of turning to gold, anything I get my hands on turns to crap."
- "I'm really backward around people. Whenever I'm around them, I just know that I'm going to say or do the wrong thing."
- "Maybe I'm misreading him. When it comes to figuring out if men are attracted to me, my track record stinks. I'm a terrible judge of character."

These statements, like the many positive and negative things you may tell yourself about yourself, reflect your *self-concept,* which is comprised of how you see yourself and who you believe yourself to be now (your self-image); who you wish you were and are striving to become (your ego-ideal); and of particular importance, how you feel about yourself and how you measure up to the standards you set for yourself (your self-esteem).

There is the "Good Me"—comprised of the attitudes and behaviors that worked for you in the past and the attributes that were rewarded by others. In this category you find all that you like about yourself; whatever you perceive to be your positive characteristics and endearing qualities. You are proud of these aspects of your identity and when they are criticized or devalued by others, or when circumstances render your strong points ineffective or useless, you are stymied. For instance, if you pride yourself on your ability to come up with original ideas, but work for a bureaucracy that lives and dies by the principle of doing things the same old way, you're apt to feel as if you're hitting your head against a brick wall. Originality is not valued by such an organization, and as a result, you may feel as if *you* are not valued, becoming frustrated and dissatisfied with a job you can only fit into by giving up a cherished source of self-esteem.

Similarly, if you view being reasonable as a personal strength but are involved in an intimate relationship with someone who runs on pure emotion and "will not listen to reason," your arguments are liable to be long and extremely heated as you stick to what you know best—being logical—even though you are not getting through to your incensed partner.

The "Bad Me" is composed of any aspects of yourself that were criticized by people who were important to you, for which you were punished or which you decided were to blame for the unpleasant experiences you had. These are now the facets of your identity that you view as weaknesses, limitations, or sore spots, and, in short, anything that you label "not good enough" in any way.

As a rule, we avoid or become extremely anxious in any situation that puts the "Bad Me" to the test—job interviews in which you must appear intelligent and articulate although you are convinced that you are neither, first dates or singles functions where your sense that you are unattractive might be confirmed, taking on a project with a short deadline even though you are sure that you cannot handle pressure. The "Bad Me" is behind much of our secret keeping as well, since we will do everything in our power to prevent our deficiencies from being discovered.

The "Not Me" is just what it sounds like—thoughts, feelings and behaviors that do not fit your self-concept; beliefs and actions that are like articles of clothing you would not be "caught dead" wearing. Unfortunately, under certain circumstances, you do indeed think, say, and do things that are "not you" and more often than not feel guilty, ashamed, and disgusted for doing so.

For instance, Greg (the special education teacher who lost the encouragement and support he enjoyed when a new principal arrived at his school) was "not one to complain," but found himself spending more and more time participating in nonstop gripe sessions with his fellow teachers. And Kate's husband, Michael, was "never someone who bottled things up inside," yet he had taken to retaliating to Kate's silent treatments by withdrawing and being silently angry himself. Similarly, those of you who "would not hurt a fly" often find yourselves in the difficult position of having to choose between staying in an unsatisfying relationship or hurting your lover by ending that relationship. In situations such as these, either self-imposed or external demands keep you from being true to yourself, whittling away at your self-esteem and making it more and more difficult to feel good about yourself. There is a definite link between self-concept and unfinished business, since most of our opinions about ourselves and the messages we hear playing on a seemingly endless tape in our own minds are actually the internalized version of messages we received from others in the past.

Perhaps as a child, you could never seem to do anything perfectly enough to please a parent who was extremely critical and quick to point out any mistakes you made. Even when no mistakes could be found, rather than praising you for a job well done, your parent may have offered suggestions on how you could do even better. Incorporating those messages into your self-concept, you give birth to an "inner critic," and that internal voice—picking up where your parent left off—constantly reminds you that you can never be good enough or careful enough and that you will always make mistakes. Each time you do in fact make a mistake, the voice of your inner critic grows louder and more oppressive, until any situation in which you could make a mistake terrifies you (and when other people's hidden agendas are operating it is even worse).

You might, on the other hand, march to a different drummer entirely. Perhaps you were constantly being absolved of all responsibility for any wrongdoing during your youth, or repeatedly rewarded for flattering and being attentive to adults. "How lucky I am to have a daughter like you," your mother would say. "You treat me so well." And your mother treated you well in return. "Let this special young lady have an extra dessert tonight," said your aunt. "I'm letting my special little girl stay up past her bedtime tonight," said your father. "I bought you a new bike," your grandmother announced, "just because you are so special to me."

Or you may hear the words of an "inner judge," who was born not so much from what was said to you but as a result of what you observed going on around you and the frustration you experienced when you compared yourself to other family members or your friends. For instance, you may have had difficulty fitting into and keeping up with the in crowd at school and come to judge yourself as "less than." You may have been harshly judging yourself ever since.

Other internal voices we may carry with us and listen to include:

- **The inner oppressor** who keeps us helpless and defeated by reminding us of all that is wrong with us and all the reasons why we don't deserve more than we already have. "You are weak (uneducated, unimaginative, unattractive, incompetent, unlikable)," it tells us, "and should be grateful that you even have a job (or a relationship or a place to live), no matter how bad it seems."

- **The inner protector** sees danger around every corner and constantly talks us out of taking risks. "Don't try it," this voice says. "You are too trusting (impulsive, naive, or unprepared), to know what you are getting into and you are going to fail (get hurt, be disappointed, rejected, or ridiculed)."

- **The inner interrogator** bombards us with questions like "Why did you do that?", "Why didn't you see this coming?", and "Why does this always happen to you?" Thinly disguised accusations, these questions come with ready-made, generally self-defeating answers—"because you are stupid (a screwup, a fool, never learn, weren't paying attention)."

- **The inner victim** responds to anything that goes wrong in your life by pointing out what you did to deserve it, why you are the one to blame for it, and how you could have avoided it if only you had been something you inherently were not (stronger, smarter, prettier, not so pretty, nicer, not so nice).

- **The inner doomsayer** is joined at the hip to the little victim and never lets you forget that you are destined to be abused, taken advantage of, negated, or fooled again and again and again.

Of course, not all of your internal voices convey negative messages. Based on more positive past experiences, you may also listen to:

- **The inner teacher** who helps you put disheartening experiences into perspective and learn from them. "Okay," it says. "So things got a little out of control this time. You're an intelligent, competent, mature adult. You can sort things out and find ways to do things differently in the future."

- **The inner cheerleader** who gives you pep talks, reminds you of your strengths or past successes and encourages you to "go for it."

- **The inner friend** who remains accepting no matter what happens. "You are okay," it says. "You are essentially a good, caring, competent, worthwhile human being. So you make mistakes. So you get confused, frustrated, angry, or depressed. Those are temporary conditions, and they don't change who you really are."

The internalized messages which convey that you are not good enough the way you are may talk you out of being yourself and talk you into playing a role instead. Thus, you use hidden agendas to create and maintain a public image that you hope will convince other people that you are better than *you* think you are.

Dreading the possibility that other people will find out that you are not who you appear to be (and as a result, think less of you), you assume a defensive posture that can distort your perception of what is going on around you and prompt you to keep secrets even when it is not in your best interest.

The internal voices and their old "not good enough" messages can also talk us into using external rewards and outward trappings of success to make up for what we believe we inherently lack. Money, power, status, lovers, and many other "objects" may be used to fill the empty spaces in our self-concept. Unfortunately, these "things" are inadequate and short-lived substitutes for self-esteem. Our appetite for them is insatiable and we must constantly obtain more and more totems, bigger and better symbols of our worth. In fact, one of the reasons baffling situations may frustrate and depress us is that they are preventing us from being rewarded quickly or often enough.

Finally, we use old messages, especially those that begin with "I should have . . . ," "Why didn't I . . . ," "I'm not . . ." and "I'll never . . ." to beat ourselves up—adding to our pain, confusion, and frustration—and cause us to read more negative meanings into situations than are actually there. For instance, those loudmouthed little voices are apt to convince us that not getting an immediate response from the boss means he hated our report and will criticize us brutally once he does meet with us or that a minor spat with our lover is "the beginning of the end" and that any minute now we will be rejected completely. We always behave as if these interpretations were the gospel truth and raise the emotional ante on various interactions, prompting us to give up too soon, put up with unsatisfying situations for too long, and employ hidden agendas more often than is in our best interest.

What Are You Telling Yourself About Yourself?

Fortunately, you can change what you tell yourself about yourself and learn to talk back to those little voices, revising the old messages to fit the realities of who you are and what you are capable of today. Of course, you will not be able to do that until you know what you tell yourself about yourself when it comes time to choose between a hidden agenda and an open one. So, the next time you encounter an anxiety-provoking situation, stop and ask yourself:

RECALL EXERCISE 5

What am I telling myself about myself right now?

Am I telling myself that I can't handle this situation/ reminding myself of how poorly I have handled such situations in the past?

Am I worrying about whether or not I am good enough to succeed in this situation?

Am I feeling as if I must keep this person from finding out something about me?

When have I told myself things like this before?

Is this situation *really* the same as that one?

Who told me these things in the past?

What were they actually referring to?

How are the circumstances different than they were then?

How am I different than I was then?

What else could I reasonably and accurately tell myself now?

If I was to turn my put-downs into a pep talk, what would I say?

Trying to Make the World the Way You Expect It to Be

The final agenda items we can get in touch with during baffling situations are our expectations and assumptions about what is *supposed* to happen in certain situations and how other people *should* think, feel, and behave.

You can begin to get a sense of what some of those expectations are by marking the points between the two extremes on the following continuums, which represent your personal opinions.

The World Is:

SAFE   **UNSAFE**

The Things that Happen to Me Are Apt to Be:

GOOD   **BAD**

People Are Basically:

TRUSTWORTHY	**UNTRUSTWORTHY**
ALTRUISTIC	**SELFISH**
INDEPENDENT & SELF-RELIANT	**DEPENDENT & CONFORMING**
RATIONAL & IN CONTROL	**CONTROLLED BY IRRATIONAL FORCES**
UNIQUE	**THE SAME**
SIMPLE	**COMPLEX**

What do the points you have marked mean in terms of your present-day thoughts, feelings, actions, and agendas? They mean that you will expect and even look for certain things to happen to you; that you will bring certain preconceived notions into most, if not all, situations and when your ideas about what is supposed to happen and how people should behave do not fit the realities of those situations, you will become anxious, confused, frustrated, and defensive.

Indeed, our expectations are often the source of our most extreme overreactions. For instance, believing that people should be responsible and consider each other's needs and feelings as well as their own, your discovery that someone has failed to make more coffee after drinking the last cup (which you would never do) can set off a ten-minute tirade on how sick and tired you are of the irresponsible and inconsiderate people who work in your office. Similarly, if the heated argument that ensues when a husband learns that his wife has registered for college courses, in hopes of completing the degree she abandoned when she married him, turns into a raging battle followed by days of tense silence and sulking, that conflict is not just about how much the course will cost or who will watch the kids while she is at school. Instead, the couple is fighting over an element of their world-view that is one of the most common sources of strife in marriages and intimate relationships—how they expect people who love each other to treat each other. He thinks, *She should have talked this over with me before she made her decision, because that is what people who care about each other are supposed to do.* They both react to their unmet (and unexpressed) expectations with anger and outrage.

Even when interactions turn out *better* than you expected, you will feel uncomfortable, perhaps saying to yourself, "This is too good to be true," or "There must be a catch" and nervously waiting for the other shoe to drop. And because of your preconceived notions, you may miss or talk yourself out of seeing vital elements of certain interactions—as many women who are sexually harassed in the workplace do. Because they do not expect sexual overtures to be made by their bosses, colleagues, or clients and make a concerted effort themselves to be all business during the business day, they do not see the early, usually subtle signs of sexual interest they encounter, or tell themselves that they are reading too much into the situation and, as a result, do nothing about it. Based on their own preconceived notions, the libidinous boss, colleague, or client interprets this nonresponse to mean that the woman is or at least might be receptive to their advances. A cat-and-mouse game ensues, with each party using hidden-agenda maneuvers—he to reduce the chance of receiving a "no" answer or "to cover his ass" in case she accuses him of sexually harassing her, and she to avoid the embarrassment or other repercussions that might result from accusing him of doing something that she can't be sure he *is* doing (since she still "can't believe he would actually come on to me at work"). On the day reality reaches out and slaps her in the face, she is shocked and "taken completely off guard," handling the situation poorly and paying dearly for her lack of awareness and inability to "see the writing on the wall."

Our expectations get us into these and other kinds of trouble when they are rigid, prompting us to classify everything as black or white and everyone as good or bad. When this occurs, we cannot comfortably and effectively deal with ambiguity—the shades of gray that color most of our real-life experiences (and all baffling situations). Also, whether rigid or not, we tend to believe that our viewpoint is the one and only, right and acceptable, frame of reference. This, of course, makes other people's behavior all the more baffling and anxiety-provoking and makes interactions more frustrating and emotionally charged than they would otherwise be.

But mostly, our expectations and assumptions get us into hot water because we think others should be who we want them to be and we feel outraged when they are not. We automatically assume that we are *entitled* to a certain kind of treatment (kindness, honesty, respect for our authority, sensitivity to our feelings), and we automatically become hurt or angry when we are not treated that way. And we automatically talk ourselves into doing things that may actually not be in our best interest—for instance, leading an isolated life and alienating everyone around us because we *expect* people to hurt and betray us.

What were you expecting? To prevent your expectations from ensnaring you in countless emotionally charged situations, you can start uncovering the preconceived notions and assumptions that may be distorting your perception of and dictating your reactions to what is going on around you.

After you next encounter a situation that "drives you up a wall" or interact with someone who "makes your hair stand on end" or feel as if "nothing is going the way it is supposed to," you can get at the expectations and assumptions that are upping the emotional ante on the interaction by giving free rein to your imagination and taking a few minutes to complete the following sentences:

1. How can he be so . . .
2. What gives him the right to . . .
3. Why does she think she has to . . .
4. Why can't they see that . . .
5. They have some nerve to . . .

Take a good look at what you've written. In your disenchanted phrases, you will clearly see what you are expecting and assuming about that situation or person and how those unmet and possibly unrealistic expectations are affecting your emotional state and ability to cope with the situation.

With practice, you will soon be able to tell that unmet expectations are influencing your reading of an interaction while the interaction is going on.

No One Is "Tuned In" All of the Time

If your head is throbbing or you are ready to toss this book across the room and shout, "There is no way that I'm going to examine myself under a microscope before every little thing I say or do," take heart. That is by no means what I am suggesting. In fact, if you had to stop and thoroughly analyze everything that went on around you, look for the reason behind everything you do or treat every situation as if you were encountering it for the first time, you would be immobilized and unable to function in the real world. Acting automatically and reacting in a characteristic manner based on what you have learned from past experience provides you with a much-needed shortcut that makes the complexities of daily living more manageable.

However, whenever you want to interpret events from a more rational perspective, turn down the volume on your inner voices (using techniques you will find in Chapter 8), and try some new responses other than your characteristic ones (including those I suggest in Chapter 9), you will also want to examine what's on your agenda.

5

Does Your Past History Repeat Itself?

The Unfinished Business of Childhood

When Howard, thirty-two, met Beth, a twenty-seven-year-old bank manager, he was the manager and part owner of a popular nightclub, earning a substantial salary and enjoying the status that came along with being on a first-name basis with both his prestigious clientele and the famous recording artists who performed at the club. As was his style with women he found attractive and believed to be "classy and sophisticated," Howard pulled out all the stops to impress Beth. "She loved the royal treatment I gave her," he insisted. In fact, assuming that she judged him by what he had to show for himself, he sometimes thought that she loved "the finer things in life" he offered her more than she loved him.

As a result, when he sold his share of the nightclub and over a two-year period opened three gourmet fast-food restaurants, Howard went out of his way to maintain his extravagant, jet-set lifestyle, telling himself that he was doing so for Beth's sake. He said, "Beth saw me as a successful businessman, a hot shot who went first class all the way. I wasn't looking forward to the day she found out that the businesses were draining me dry and I didn't have an extra dime to my name." Believing that when that day came Beth would dump him, Howard postponed its arrival by keeping his precarious financial situation a secret—pretending that his shops were thriving and giving Beth the same "royal treatment" he had given her before he went into business for himself.

Although Howard made this decision without consulting Beth, he began to resent her for "forcing" him to make it. "It bugged me that I couldn't talk about what was going on with the businesses," he explained. "It was such a chore to put on this happy face and have conversations about everything except what was really on my mind." It never occurred to him that Beth, with her banking background and financial expertise, might actually have been able to help him sort out and solve his business problems. And even when keeping up the "everything is fine, fine, fine" pretense began using up more energy than Howard had to spare, he did not disclose the truth to Beth. Instead, he spent less time with her and "told more lies to explain why I wasn't seeing her."

However, watching his relationship with Beth deteriorate—which was precisely what he had hoped to avoid—was "small potatoes" compared to the anger and outrage he felt each time he "threw away money" to take Beth to a high-priced restaurant or to a prestigious one-hundred-dollar per person charity gala or on overnight getaways to nearby luxury hotels.

"Beth is too damn status conscious," he complained bitterly. *Why should I go to the poor-house for someone so shallow and materialistic? One of these days, I'm just going to tell her to take a hike, to go find herself some other sucker to support her expensive tastes and "gimme, gimme" lifestyle.*

Perhaps you recognize that Howard is doing what Eddie did—unwittingly projecting his own undesirable qualities onto someone else. Unbeknownst to Howard, he was using Beth to help him maintain a lifestyle he could not afford without feeling guilty or getting angry at himself for living beyond his means. He simply got angry at Beth instead. He'd convinced himself that the dire straits he was in were all due to Beth, and the money he'd been spending on her. He finally confronted her with "the facts," only to discover that those were not the facts at all.

Beth let Howard rant and rave until he ran out of things to say. Then she laughed. "For an intelligent man, you can be incredibly stupid," she said. "I work for the bank that handles your accounts. I know exactly how your businesses are doing. What I couldn't understand was why you wouldn't talk about it. Every time I asked, you changed the subject, so I stopped asking. That didn't mean I didn't care. And it certainly isn't my fault that you didn't listen to the hundreds of times I said that going to fancy restaurants or clubs that charge ten dollars per drink or this month's hot vacation spot wasn't important to me. This 'lifestyles of the rich and famous' thing is your fantasy, not mine. I'd be perfectly happy to stay home, watch videos, and eat pizza. In fact, there were plenty of times that that was all I wanted to do."

Beth's reaction took Howard completely by surprise. Her words were those he least expected to hear, and once they sank in he realized that "I had blown everything out of proportion and made myself more and more miserable over things that *weren't happening anywhere except in my own head.*" They had, however, happened to Howard in the past. All of the thoughts and feelings he projected onto Beth were part of his old agenda—the internal file that contains every significant lesson you ever learned about yourself, other people, and how to live in the real world; which needs and wishes are safe to have and how to fulfill them; as well as what consequences to fear and how to avoid them. Like a computer's memory bank, your psyche is filled with billions of bytes of this previously encoded data. As you saw on a smaller scale in the last chapter, when those internal files merge with incoming information about your immediate circumstances, you blow things out of proportion and raise the emotional ante on already distressing situations—as Howard did—driving yourself crazy over something that exists primarily in your mind.

"I'm your basic nobody, a poor jerk without an extra dime to my name," Howard said. "A lousy businessman," he called himself, "incompetent." In addition to bombarding himself with these negative messages day in and day out, when I first met him, Howard was spending nearly every waking moment in a state of anxiety. Convinced that he would soon be forced to declare bankruptcy, he constantly bemoaned the fact that he was "working harder than I ever have and I don't have a damn thing to show for it."

Yet, Howard had three gourmet fast-food restaurants (two that were holding their own and one that was actually turning a profit) to show for his effort. What's more, he hardly lived like a pauper. He owned a home, a car, and luxuries like designer clothes, membership to an exclusive health club, and a small sailboat—things that other people truly could not afford. Yes, while getting his businesses off the ground, he had to pass up a great deal on a classic car, forgo the time-share condo in the Caribbean, and deprive himself of a ski trip to Switzerland. However, that hardly constituted living from hand to mouth—which was how Howard described his current financial status. No matter how many times these facts were pointed out to him, he treated them as if they were meaningless. His old agenda prevented him from seeing what he did have, while keeping him painfully aware of what he lacked.

Howard grew up the middle child and only son in an upper-middle-class, status-conscious family. They were living beyond their means, but that never seemed to matter. "Living the good life and making sure that everyone knew you could afford to was what my family was into," Howard commented. But Howard was into it as well. At the most fundamental level, he adopted the belief that *obtaining more, bigger, and better symbols of success was the only true measure of being a success.*

Following the example set by his parents, by adolescence all of Howard's friends were the offspring of the town's wealthiest and most highly respected families. He began to realize that, appearance aside, his own family didn't fall into that category. While his friends had seemingly limitless amounts of spending money, he had to supplement his modest allowance with earnings from odd jobs. His friends also stood to inherit vast fortunes before their thirtieth birthdays. He knew that he had no such inheritance awaiting him. "I was always a couple of steps behind them and racing to catch up," he said, inadvertently touching upon another crucial element of his old agenda. Since he came to believe that because his friends could "do anything they wanted without worrying about every penny they spent," and he could not, he gave birth to an inner judge that would bombard him with self-defeating messages throughout his life: *he was not as good as the others were, and would not be until he somehow managed to have as much as they did and live the lifestyle they led.*

At sixteen—when fitting in with and being like one's peers seems vitally important—Howard made a decision "to be comfortable enough by the time I turned thirty to have the finer things in life without worrying about being able to afford them."

Unfortunately, Howard had not lived up to his own expectation. Two years after his deadline, not only wasn't he "set for life," but because he had used his savings to start his businesses and those businesses were not yet making enormous profits, he could not even afford all of the "finer things in life" that he wanted. While someone without Howard's old agenda might consider these conditions to be temporary and devote his energy to finding ways to make the businesses more profitable, Howard fretted and stewed, spinning his wheels, labeling himself a failure with a capital "F," and blaming his unhappiness on Beth.

Like Howard, when we are unaware of our old agendas, we jump to conclusions that are not only inaccurate and detrimental to our lives and relationships, but also keep us from changing ourselves or our circumstances for the better.

We do not have to do this, of course. We can take the time to ask ourselves what's on our agendas *during* baffling situations, using the questions in the last chapter. However, to truly understand the answers we come up with and complete unfinished business that *repeatedly* gets in our way, we must dig deeper.

Although a single chapter in a single book cannot be expected to shed light on all or even most of anyone's old agenda, the information and self-awareness exercises you will find in the remainder of this chapter can get you moving in the right direction as you begin your quest for the past experiences and relationships that continue to have a significant impact on your life today.

Old Agendas

Each of us is an intricately woven tapestry. Our identities are built slowly. In and out of the warp laid by our families, we constantly weave in new threads colored by our experiences with countless people and events that are significant to us in any way. We have experiences that enhance our sense of competence and self-worth, that convince us that we have talents and strengths, can take risks and succeed, interact with people and be liked. Unfortunately, we also have experiences and get involved in relationships that create quite the opposite effect. Whether good or bad, painful or pleasurable, self-enhancing or self-defeating, the attitudes and beliefs we developed as a result of our noteworthy past experiences and relationships are incorporated into our *old agendas*.

As they certainly did for Howard, those old agendas in turn influence how we interpret and respond to *new* situations, and can to a certain extent even determine the sorts of situations we get ourselves into. Consequently, the most meaningful (in both a negative and positive sense) experiences in our personal life histories have happened not just once but many times over. Like the story line of a novel or play, certain themes run through our lives. In order to understand the influence of our old agendas, it helps to recognize the themes that seem to recur in our lives.

Take some time to think about the following questions. You may find it helpful to put some of your thoughts down on paper. You may also want to get some input from others, preferably people who know you well and whom you trust.

RECALL EXERCISE 6

Under what circumstances do you find yourself thinking, "Why does this always happen to me?"

What issues (making commitments, relationships that seem like the right ones but aren't, getting the credit you deserve) seem to show up in your life over and over again?

What situations do you tend to shy away from? What sorts of messes do you repeatedly get yourself into? What have you repeatedly promised yourself never to do or let happen again?

Think of a recent dilemma you faced. Then think back to the last time you encountered a dilemma like it and the time before that and the time before that. What did these situations have in common?

What are your pet peeves, the situations or other people's actions that drive you up a wall? Think of a half-dozen times when you encountered them. In addition to the irritation they caused, what else did those situations have in common?

Depending upon how much thought you have already given to the déjà vu–like experiences in your life, you may quickly begin to see patterns emerge. And even if those patterns are not crystal clear, you will get your first inkling of how you may be unwittingly transferring your past history onto people and situations in the present.

This process is most noticeable in your dealings with authority figures. In the presence of people who are more powerful than you are, who seem to be in control of your fate or have the wherewithal to reward or punish you, you may become a nervously squirming child again and attempt to win others' approval or protect yourself from punishment—often using the same methods you used as a child.

You may already be aware that you do this, but just in case you are tempted to say "No, I don't," take a moment to remember what you used to do to get your parents' attention and approval. Did you point out something you had done that you thought they would be proud of, engage them in a conversation about their favorite topic, tattle on a sibling, flatter them? And how did you behave when you had done something they did not like or were angry about? Did you cry, try to cover up your misdeed, explain or justify your mistakes, confess before they could find out the truth from someone else, get "cute" or silly, physically avoid them for as long as possible? If you compare what you did and how you were feeling then with your recent dealings with your boss, your doctor, a police officer, or any other authoritative person, the similarities may astound you.

What's more, many of us are so loyal to our old agendas that, regardless of who or what we are facing, we act and react as if we were spellbound. For instance, one of my patients, a young woman named Patty, could not bring herself to let a kind, handsome coworker know that she was attracted to him. She could say to me or to her friends that she was interested in him and wished he would ask her out. She even knew that he had expressed interest in her—since more than one of her coworkers had mentioned it. She even decided that she would smile at him or start a casual conversation the next time she saw him. But she never did. Indeed, she went out of her way to deflect his attention—never once looking in his direction during a staff meeting, removing herself from his line of vision by searching for something in her bottom drawer and even waiting for the next elevator if he was about to get on the one that just arrived. "I know it's absolutely insane," she said. "But it's like some stranger took over and compelled me to do those things."

That stranger was Patty's old agenda. In her youth, Patty had faded into the woodwork during the frequent battles between her mother and her father, also staying out of their way afterward because, even though she needed to be comforted and reassured, she knew from experience that, if she sought what she needed, her Mom and Dad would tell her to go away and leave them alone. As a result, she had come to believe that *letting people know that you want affection or attention from them will lead to rejection,* and this past programming was so powerful that it compelled her to do the opposite of what she wished to do: forcing her not to draw attention to herself when attention was precisely what she wanted.

Although not necessarily in the same way Patty's did, when your old agenda is calling the shots, you act as if *what once happened is still happening*—repeatedly bumping and banging your original sore spots and reinforcing your old attitudes and beliefs.

RECALL EXERCISE 7

What is your earliest memory?

What were the favorite times of your life?

What were some of the most difficult times in your life?

Think about these questions casually, playfully. Do not concentrate on finding the "right" answer, but instead notice your first impressions, any random images that pop into your mind. Jot them down on scraps of paper or in a notebook, taking several days to gather your thoughts if you wish.

Then sit down, look over your notes and fill in any details that come to mind—images of the people involved; the ideas and emotions you associate with those times; what you were doing; what other people were doing; what those times seemed to be about (control, for instance, or accomplishing something or being close to someone) and so on. Be as loose as possible, letting your pen flow across the page and seeing what words appear. They are apt to be quite telling.

Your earliest memory, even if it is hazy or incomplete, frequently uncovers the cornerstone in the foundation upon which your identity is built. At the very least, it is likely to reveal a fundamental element of your old agenda that you may in one way or another be reenacting to this day. Such was the case for Howard, whose earliest memory involved listening to stories told by Marlena, the live-in housekeeper who took care of him during the first six years of his life.

"Marlena could be very 'cool'," Howard recalled. "But basically she was a really tough, no-nonsense lady. She was big, for one thing, and had a husky, almost masculine voice. Even her laugh had sort of a hard edge to it. She fought in the French Resistance during World War II and had been through all kinds of rough times since then. She talked about it as much as you asked her to and some of her stories were better than the war movies you saw on TV. That's the main thing I remember about her, the stories she told and that she was a big believer in fighting, you know, standing up for yourself against any odds. I guess I remember that because I wasn't much of a fighter myself."

Actually Howard was not a fighter at all—which turned out to be the real reason Marlena told him so many war stories as well as the reason for the link between past and present. You see, young Howard was constantly getting ambushed by various neighborhood or schoolyard bullies, and since there were usually more than one and they were bigger than he, it seemed ludicrous to fight back. "If they wanted my lunch money, I gave it to them," he said. "Sometimes I bribed them with candy or toys, but they generally got in a few punches anyway." Whenever he came home with a new bruise or grass stains on his clothes, Marlena would sit him down, tell him another tale of her French Resistance activity and encourage him to fight back. He never did and Marlena eventually lost patience with him. "Tomorrow you fight back," she told him, giving Howard her most menacing I-mean-business glare, "or don't bother coming home."

Being a five-year-old and in awe of this woman who had been the most consistent source of love and attention in his life thus far, Howard took what she said at face value and sincerely believed that if he did not do as she said, he would not be allowed back into his home and family. Yet he was equally frightened by the prospect of taking on the bullies who outnumbered and outmatched him. How did he resolve his dilemma? *He got beaten by the bullies as usual and then lied to Marlena.* Indeed, his tale of the incredible fighting he did was nearly as colorful as her war stories. She congratulated him enthusiastically and even gave him an extra scoop of ice cream at dinner that evening. For as long as she was with the family, Howard continued to deceive Marlena, both by telling her tall tales and by simply hiding the fact that he had had another run-in with the bullies. As a result, Howard learned a lesson that would remain with him for years to come—*to save face and avoid being rejected by people who are important to you, you must never let them know about your weaknesses or the situations you cannot handle on your own.* This was, of course, the element of his old agenda that convinced him to keep his precarious financial situation hidden from Beth.

Your earliest memory may not lead to as direct or significant a connection as Howard's, but it is a place to start—the first piece in the complex jigsaw puzzle picture of who you are today.

The favorite times in your life serve as another puzzle piece—one that may tell you what ideas, emotional states, and life circumstances you are trying to recapture or hold on to in the present. Continuing to use Howard as an example, let's look at what he had to say on this subject. "I guess my favorite times were during childhood," he recalled. "Everything was a lot easier then and I don't remember worrying about anything. I can tell you that one of my favorite things to do when I was little was to put on my dad's hat and driving gloves, go into the garage, get behind the wheel of his car and pretend I was cruising down some back road at ninety miles an hour." What Howard pretended to do was one of the things his father actually did to unwind and one way Howard identified with or "became like" this important person in his life.

Another cherished memory of Howard's also occurred during his youth and involved feeling close and connected to his father by sharing his interest in the finer things in life. "I probably knew more about fine wines, classic cars, exotic vacation spots and state-of-the-art stereo equipment than any ten-year-old in America," Howard said proudly. "Those were the things my dad and I talked about. It was sort of a game we played. I'd go through his magazines as soon as they arrived and then that night when he was reading them, he'd quiz me on things. It was this special thing between just the two of us."

Perhaps you can already identify the ways these fondly remembered past experiences continue to influence Howard today. From wanting his life to be easy and comfortable to wanting not to worry about money or anything else, from continuing to build his identity on what he had to show for himself to using the royal treatment to impress and be close to people, he is trying to get back to the best times in his life. And if you look closely at yourself, you may discover that you are—perhaps less dramatically—trying to do this too.

Conversely, the distressing experiences and difficult times you remember provide clues to what you do *not* want today, the circumstances that you will go to almost any length to avoid. "Hands down, the worst time in my life was my senior year in high school," Howard sighed. "My parents all of a sudden decided that it was time for me to learn 'the true meaning of a dollar,' as they put it. They bought me a clunker of a car and wouldn't let me drive it until I earned the money to pay for my own insurance. So I got this horrible job bussing tables in a diner and while all of my friends were having the best year of their lives, I was working and praying they didn't come into the diner and see me. I must have told a million lies that year to explain why I couldn't go places with them and when they did find out the truth, they never let me live it down. I swore I'd never let that happen again, but sometimes I feel like that's exactly what's happening, especially during the lunch rush at one of my shops when my dishwasher doesn't show up and I'm up to my elbows in greasy pots and pans.''

As you can see, a bit of playful ribbing by his wealthy friends seemed to be the most humiliating moment of Howard's entire life—in retrospect. When combined with his sense that he did not and would never measure up to his friends, Howard's determination *never* to be looked down upon and ridiculed like that again became a driving force in his life.

In addition, our memories of unpleasant experiences often include the actions we took to cope with those situations—and which we, in all probability, still continue to use. Thus Patty, who faded into the woodwork during the terrifying times when her parents were fighting, continues to make herself invisible when her handsome coworker is nearby. Similarly, Jeff, who escaped his girlfriend Carol's intimate overtures by talking about old girlfriends, problems at work, the plumbing that needed fixing or any other untimely topic he could come up with, once dodged his smothering mother's invasions of privacy by changing the subject of conversation to almost anything that did not directly involve him.

For the sake of clarity, many of the examples and anecdotes you find in this book trace a direct route from one or two significant past experiences to hidden and automatic agendas being employed in the present. This may have led you to believe that a single event is the sole source of most people's present-day problems. This is not the case.

There is no simple cause and effect. No two people travel the exact same path from the day they are born until the day they die. All of us have different experiences with different people at different times in our lives. We interpreted those experiences differently, coped with stressful situations differently, attributed great significance to events that someone else might have deemed unimportant and so on.

For instance, Howard's older sister Reba, although raised in the same environment, was not the least bit status conscious and did not care one whit about what she had to show for herself. When she looked around her and saw how difficult it would be to keep up with the rich kids, she decided that she did *not want* to be like them and avoided that crowd. She eschewed her parents' values instead of identifying with them and was so good at being "just plain folks" that when she brought friends home with her from college, they were shocked by the sight of her huge home and her family's life-style. This did not mean that Reba had no old agenda. She did. It was simply different than her brother's.

As you could see, Reba did not engage in the same behaviors she witnessed earlier in her life. You may not either. In fact, some of us decided at a very early age never to do or be like our parents or allow ourselves to get into situations resembling those we encountered in the past. For instance, those of us who grew up in families that were disrupted by conflict, who were hurt by our parents' sometimes violent outbursts or who participated in the family-wide cover-up of abusive behavior, tend to fear and avoid conflict and anger. "I will not be angry," we decided back then and still bottle up our hostile feelings, suffering various physical and psychological symptoms because those feelings are festering inside of us. "I will never be violent," we declared in the past and since we have yet to hit anyone or break things, we feel we've kept that promise. However, the hostile feelings we try so desperately to suppress leak out anyway, so we may be violent in more subtle ways—with disapproving looks, silent rebuffs, sarcasm, humiliation, love withdrawn, or passive-aggressive behavior. Obviously, doing the opposite of what we once saw or did is still an automatic response influenced by our old agendas—and not a free choice.

Going Back to the Source

Although early experiences with our parents or other family members are not the only ones that influence us, the fact is that for each of us, growing up in a particular family leaves an indelible imprint upon us. This imprint is not necessarily negative, mind you, but it is there and, whether we consciously recognize it or not, provides us with one unique lens through which we perceive and react to the circumstances we encounter today.

Stephanie, the problem-solving employee at the import company who always covered for her incompetent boss—back in the Introduction of this book—grew up in a big, tightly knit extended family. "My grandparents lived with us," she explained. "And I don't think a day passed without a couple of aunts, uncles, or cousins coming by to visit or help take care of my brother, Bobby, who was bedridden because of a heart disease. Every holiday, you could expect a crowd of at least fifty, and every summer we rented two big houses at the shore and the whole clan went down there for a week." Stephanie's relatives served not only as her immediate family's social circle, but as their support system as well. "If you needed something fixed, you called Uncle Joe," she continued. "Aunt Mary did everyone's taxes. My dad loaned out his truck more than he drove it, since someone always needed help moving something somewhere. And everyone was always trading things. You could feel right at home anywhere since there was a good chance that something that used to be yours was sitting on the floor or hanging on the windows at someone else's house."

Stephanie's family was more than tightly knit. It was a closed system in which all but the most extraordinary needs were fulfilled *without* outside intervention. In all likelihood, Stephanie's parents would not have been able to care for

Bobby at home if it had not been for the help they received from their relatives. And in the aftermath of Bobby's death, all those aunts, uncles, and cousins came to the rescue, preparing meals, cleaning house, caring for Stephanie and her sisters and doing everything they could to help the family through the crisis.

No one in Stephanie's family ever said, "We have to solve all of our problems ourselves." No one ever verbally instructed her not to seek outside help when she got into a bind. They modeled that behavior instead. For anything short of a medical emergency, one family member or another stepped in and took care of the problem. Indeed, if they had a family crest, the motto emblazoned across it would have read, "We Handle Things Ourselves," and Stephanie—who, as you will read more about in the next chapter, frequently took on the tasks no one else wanted to do at work and rarely revealed that she had a problem until it had truly reached crisis proportions—was still living by it.

Our families were the first place where we *belonged*, and one of our earliest bouts of anxiety stemmed from the awareness of how utterly alone and unprotected we would be without them. To avoid such an unfathomable fate, we did whatever was necessary to fit into our families, taking our cues from every interaction that occurred and every nuance of daily behavior we observed. *"This is what members of my family think, feel, and do,"* was the message that took root in our unconscious minds each time we witnessed certain actions and reactions. *"Since I am also a member of this family, I will think, feel, and behave this way too."* And so we, like Stephanie, automatically emulated these behaviors, adopting the attitudes that went with them.

Through *identification* (becoming like the people who are or were important to us), *adaptation* (the ways we coped with unexpected, frustrating, or frightening situations), and *internalization* (wholeheartedly believing and adopting as our own the messages about ourselves conveyed to us by others), we accumulated attitudes and beliefs about ourselves, other people, and life in general which we never really forget.

Among the many things we absorbed were certain attitudes, beliefs, and behavior patterns that would continue to influence us each and every time that we were called upon to choose between an open agenda with a direct approach and a hidden one. You see, secret keeping is a subject families teach exceedingly well.

FAMILY SECRETS

All families keep secrets. Some families are more secretive than others, of course. And all have at least slightly different methods for concealing or misrepresenting certain feelings, both within the family and from outsiders. In some instances a family *myth* (We are a happy family. Daddy works late so you can have nice things. Mommy has a headache.) stands in the place of an unpleasant truth. (We don't get along. Daddy is at his girlfriend's house. Mommy's diet pills are wearing off.) In other instances, attention may be directed from a frightening fact. ("Let's go get ice cream," Mom says cheerfully after Dad has finished smashing the porch furniture and driven off swearing never to return.) Or facts may be repackaged to make them more palatable. (We weren't yelling because we were angry, just raising our voices a little because we were excited.) In general, the more damaging or frightening the information being concealed, the greater the lengths family members will go to conceal it—and the more compelled we will be to maintain the cover-up.

The secrets families keep fall into three general categories, identified as:

- **Unmentionable Indiscretions:** This information is not acknowledged within the family. It may involve problems between parents (including physical abuse, infidelity, financial woes, and so on) which are concealed from the children, or topics that are off-limits for everyone, such as the fact that Grandma is getting senile, that Uncle Ed touches his nieces in places they would prefer not to be touched, that sister Suzie has manic-depressive illness or that brother Billy managed to obtain an expensive gold chain that he could not possibly afford to buy. Also falling into this category are taboos about openly expressing feelings, such as disappointment or anger, and thoughts that differ from or contradict those of other family members.

· **For Our Ears Only:** This information is concealed from outsiders and often involves collusion between family members to maintain a happy family facade. These are the secrets that give us our first inklings about "little white lies," embellishing to make certain circumstances seem rosier than they really are, creating the "right" impression and other staples that will later become part of our hidden-agenda repertoire. Extremely stressful when the secret involves serious problems like child abuse, domestic violence, addictions, or sexual misconduct, the "dirty linen" we do not air in public may also include information about temporary financial setbacks, details of arguments that took place inside the home, facts that would embarrass or belittle another family member, and so on.

· **Time-lapsed Data:** That a child is adopted, the seriousness of a family member's illness, confirmation that marital problems do indeed exist, or the details of what really happened on the night those police officers came to the door are a few examples of information that is temporarily hidden from one or more family members. The person who has the information (usually a parent) withholds it until they decide others (usually children) are ready to hear it. Sometimes children are the withholders, as you well know if you ever waited for your parents to be in a good mood before showing them your report card or still have not told them exactly what you were doing in the rec room with the boy next door.

The nature and content of your family's secrets, the rules about *what kinds* of information is and is not safe to reveal and who within or outside the family can be trusted with which facts or feelings are apt to be the very same rules you apply to all of your personal and professional relationships. In addition, if you take a close look, you will also see your family's influence on the types of secret-keeping methods you use today.

RECALL EXERCISE 8

Of the defensive maneuvers, power plays, or self-deceptions you use on a regular basis, which did you observe your parents, siblings, friends, or other influential people in your life using?

Under what circumstances did these people employ those hidden agendas?

From these role models, what did you learn about practicing the art of deception (including when it was okay to keep secrets and what kinds of secrets it was okay to keep)?

Today, which maneuvers, when used by others to manipulate, control, or deceive you, create the most anxiety or frustration for you?

Where have you encountered those maneuvers before?

How did you feel *then* about yourself, the person with the hidden agenda and the situation you were in?

What was the outcome of that interaction (i.e., did it enable you to or prevent you from fulfilling your own agenda)?

How did you react?

When was the first time you can remember employing the defensive maneuvers that you now use on a regular basis?

What was going on?

What were you trying to avoid or obtain?

How effective was your ploy?

In what other situations did you use a maneuver and what lesson did you learn about when, how, and with whom to rely on hidden agendas?

Getting Out from Under Your Old Agendas

Although far from exhaustive, the exploration of old agendas found in this chapter was intended to bring you several steps closer to changing yourself or your circumstances so that you can handle baffling situations without driving yourself crazy. By bringing past experiences and influences into clearer focus, you get more useful answers when you ask yourself what's on your agenda. By recognizing where and how you think, feel, and act like the person you once were instead of the person you are now, you get the chance to remind yourself of how much you've grown—and how many more things you can do *now* to cope with a baffling situation than you were able to do in the past. Your options increase tenfold and the idea of using one of them (instead of your same old maneuvers) is far less frightening than ever before.

Now that this tenacious obstacle to changing yourself or your circumstances is on the way to being dismantled, let's move on to another—the rules and expectations that dictate what happens in your personal and professional relationships.

6

Relationships That Bind

The Psychological Contracts We Make and Break

Now that you know more about psychological agendas, let's take another look at that minidrama I described way back in the Introduction—the one in which Bart, the newly hired development director for an import company, was "getting away with murder"; Stephanie (about whom you've just read) was "running herself ragged" managing Bart's department; and David, who as head of the new products division could have resolved the problem, was doing nothing about it.

Folie à Trois

Bart, forty-two, working on his third marriage and his fifth "new" career, had a relatively uncomplicated, all-purpose psychological agenda. It revolved around the premise that the best way to get what he wanted was to manipulate other people into doing for him what he should be doing for himself. Sometimes he achieved this end by "digging up dirt" to use against those he was attempting to manipulate. Sometimes he played on the sympathies of old friends. But most of the time, he simply assumed the role of "village idiot," feigning confusion and helplessness.

In fact, he had been honing his approach since childhood. The "klutzy, absent-minded" youngest child in an achievement-oriented family, Bart never seemed to do anything well enough to satisfy his perfectionistic parents. However, he was protected from their wrath and criticism by his oldest sister, who stepped in either to fix or cover up his mistakes. As a result, his self-esteem was spared the damaging message that neglecting to do things or doing them poorly were signs of irresponsibility and incompetence. Instead, his old agenda told him that absent-mindedness and being a klutz were endearing qualities which prompted certain people to feel sorry for him and do his bidding. Over the years Bart used his keen intelligence and abundant charm to develop better ways to maneuver others into helping him out. He also had an uncanny knack for finding people to assume the role his sister had played during childhood. At the import company, that person was Stephanie.

"I can't see the point of waiting around for Bart to make messes I'll have to clean up anyway," Stephanie said. "It's a lot easier to just go ahead and handle things on my own." As you may recall, Stephanie's old agenda included the idea that handling things on her own was the best response to most situations.

Throughout her twelve years with the company Stephanie had always given 110 percent, doing more than was expected of her and taking on unofficial duties in addition to her official ones. Over the years her efficiency, dedication, and ability to predict which new products would be "winners" so intrigued David that when he became the head of the new products division, he took Stephanie with him as his administrative assistant. She assumed more and more responsibility, never seeming to mind that David constantly poured out his personal problems to her, expected her to work on evenings and weekends, and periodically took credit for her ideas. It did not seem to bother her that her new job titles and functions rarely came with more than minuscule salary increases.

Although you might find this lopsided arrangement intolerable, Stephanie barely noticed that she was giving a great deal more than she was getting in return. This, too, reflected an old agenda. Stephanie had become self-reliant and hyperresponsible at an early age because the lion's share of her parents' time and attention were devoted to keeping her chronically ill brother alive. As soon as she was old enough, she began sharing this caretaking responsibility and no longer missed being taken care of. In fact, she much preferred to take care of others even if it meant neglecting or overburdening herself. This seemed as automatic to Stephanie as breathing.

What's more, like many efficient but not formally educated employees who know they are unlikely to move any further up the corporate ladder, Stephanie compensated for any self-doubt she had by constantly proving to herself and others that she was indispensable. Unfortunately, this crucial element of her psychological agenda made Stephanie the perfect patsy for Bart's village-idiot act.

Where was David while all this was happening? On the scene, with his head buried in the sand. He was maintaining a hefty hidden agenda of his own.

You see, the import company was owned by David's family. It was common knowledge that David's father was grooming David to take over for him when he retired. But

David was convinced that his father thought him incapable of assuming that responsibility. Indeed, David saw his father as constantly waiting to pounce on him and point out his inadequacies. He also believed that he could postpone the inevitable by *concealing his mistakes.* Hiring Bart definitely fell into that category.

Several times over the years, the volatile relationship between David and his father spontaneously combusted and David temporarily left the company. During one of these periods of estrangement, Bart, an old friend from David's college days, helped get David a job at the insurance company where he was working at the time. In addition, Bart, who was in between wives, let David stay with him and took him out drinking and carousing in order to take his mind off his troubles. During a number of these inebriated free-for-alls, David had some regrettable misadventures—all of which came back to haunt him when Bart, deeply in debt because of a failed business venture, came looking for repayment of the favor.

Playing David's sense of obligation for all it was worth and "accidentally" making references to David's misadventures while reminiscing about the good old days, Bart pushed enough buttons to convince David that he could not let his friend in need down. Even though he had originally intended to promote Stephanie into it, David offered Bart the development director's position.

Watching Bart operate, David soon regretted his decision, but he could not back down without admitting he had made a mistake and hearing about his latest failure from his father. You can imagine how relieved he felt when Stephanie stepped in to compensate for Bart's deficiencies. Each time she rescued Bart, Stephanie rescued David as well and he was truly grateful for this.

Every chance he got, David told Stephanie what a terrific job she was doing and went out of his way to say in front of others that his division would "fall apart without her." He occasionally mentioned that he was planning to approach the executive board about giving her a raise, and although he never actually did this, his encouraging words were enough to fuel Stephanie's agenda and, as a result, keep the chain reaction going.

As exploitative and potentially destructive as their circumstances may seem, at this point in Stephanie, Bart, and David's story, their relationship was not about to change. In each other and their situation, they had found a way to meet their needs, including several that they did not even know they had.

The Invisible Lifeline—Using Relationships to Fulfill Our Agendas

Just as a brand-new automatic-drip coffeemaker with all of its internal parts in working order cannot make coffee unless you plug it into a source of electricity, there are many items on our individual agendas that require input from others in order to be fulfilled. To meet certain needs, we look for the source that can supply the "electricity" we need to operate comfortably and effectively. Sometimes consciously (but more often without conscious awareness), we connect with people, groups, or organizations that seem to hold the pieces missing from the jigsaw puzzle of who we are or hope to become.

Wishing to advance professionally, you look for a mentor or network with others in the industry. Needing to talk about your concerns and receive guidance or encouragement, you seek out friends or a therapist. To satisfy your yearning for intimacy, you are drawn into a love affair or get involved in a community activity. If you are a parent, a teacher, or a nurse, your children, students, or patients provide an outlet for your need to nurture. And the organization that employs you supplies everything from a source of income to a sense of belonging.

Naturally, the person, group, or organization you turn to in hopes of fulfilling your agenda have agendas of their own. For instance, the supervisor you hope will mentor you may in fact derive satisfaction from mentoring others. Or she may think that shaping you into a model employee will make her look good in the eyes of her superiors and land her a promotion. Or she may be looking for someone to do her drudge work. Any one of these motives—whether they are out in the open, consciously concealed from you, or unconscious, and whether or not they will help or hurt you in the long run—make her agenda *compatible* with yours and a relationship is likely to be forged.

Similarly, your potential friend or mate may want intimacy, companionship, and affection, too, and be motivated to give it in order to receive it, just as you are. On the other hand, he may primarily be seeking sexual gratification or someone to mother him or to replace his ex-girlfriend or ex-wife. Again, your agendas, although not identical, are compatible and developing a relationship is possible. Where that relationship will lead you is another story entirely, but at the outset the potential for both of you to meet vital needs is present, and chances are that you will "go for it."

The same can be said for the relationship that exists between you and the organization that employs you. Any organization can provide you with a source of income, various benefits, a job title and so on because it needs workers who are qualified and willing to perform certain tasks. However, you may want to work for an organization that also fulfills your desire to move up the corporate ladder, have a certain amount of job security, or list the name of a prestigious company on your résumé. That organization may, in turn, be looking for someone with prior experience in the field; someone who will come to work on time, put in his eight hours and not "rock the boat"; or someone who will work twelve to fourteen hour days and "shake things up." If you believe you can get what you want from them and they believe they can get what they want from you, you embark upon a relationship and *expect it to continue meeting your needs as long as you continue to contribute what you "agreed" to contribute.*

As well-meaning mothers have assured their single daughters for generations, there is indeed "a lid for every pot." And, although it was not what happened at the import company, what gets cooked in that pot *can* be quite nourishing. For instance, if a brilliant but disorganized scientist teams up with an efficient but uninspired associate, together they could make a major medical breakthrough and end up winning the Nobel prize—a feat neither would have been able to accomplish alone. Likewise, if you are shy and reserved while your best friend is confident and outgoing, some of her chutzpah could rub off on you. She, in turn, might learn a thing or two from you about putting people at ease by speaking softly and listening attentively. As a result of your relationship, each of you is *more* than you were before.

In addition, you may derive pleasure from seeing the world through the eyes of someone whose point of view is quite different from your own—as parents often do while interacting with their children. And of course, when elements of your own and someone else's agendas are similar as well as compatible, you both feel understood and at ease. You get each other's jokes, know how to comfort each other, or act in concert during a crisis.

Regrettably, interlocking agendas are also responsible for:

- malingering employees (or disrespectful ones like Eddie) who manage to hang on to their jobs for years while everyone works around them;
- committee cochairpersons or partnerships in which one person is continually exploited by the other, who then takes all the glory and/or money;
- battered spouses who cling to their relationships with their abusers;
- couples who are unwilling to change anything about their relationships even though they are miserable and do little more than argue with each other;
- men and women who allow their friends to dump on them.

In each instance and many others, the relationship is held together and kept on the same seemingly senseless course because it fulfills elements of each party's *automatic* agenda. And the unconscious forces drawing them together are much more powerful than the logical, observable reasons to part company or change their relationship in any way. This was certainly the case for Bart, Stephanie, and David, whose unacknowledged and for the most part unrecognized needs were as synchronized as a Radio City Rockettes' kickline. As long as those unconscious elements of their individual agendas were being fulfilled, they would automatically maintain the relationship *as it was.*

Even though they were not aware of it, that was one of the terms in the *psychological contract* which governed their relationship; the implicit, unspoken bargain that serves as the foundation of any relationship. Most of the rules we, too, play by or the norms we live up to in our relationships are completely unconscious. Others we do know about but have never given them much conscious thought or considered whether or not they are working in our best interest. Why not take some time to do that now, exploring a psychological contract of your own while I explain psychological contracts in general.

The Psychological Contract

From the many business, personal, casual, intimate, harmonious, adversarial, troubling, or practically perfect relationships you now have, choose one that you would like to examine closely.

Then take out a sheet of paper and, holding it horizontally, draw a chart that looks like this:

Give	Get	My Priorities	Their Priorities	Talked About	Expectations	Changes

In the first wide column (labeled GIVE), list *your* contribution to the relationship: what you give to the other person, group, or organization, what you are responsible for, what you are expected to do or not do. The list can include:

- specific, tangible contributions (arrive at work on time, take out the trash, call before visiting);
- general categories (child rearing, paperwork, listening to his/her problems);
- rules you try to follow (never go to bed angry, don't disagree when others are around to hear, own up to your mistakes).

If you choose to list an intangible contribution like "be supportive" or "show affection," tack on at least one observable behavior that reflects it (for example, let him complain about his boss or remember to give a gift on birthdays and other special occasions).

After you have completed this list, fill in the second wide column (labeled GET) with things you expect to receive from the other participant in this relationship. The same general guidelines should be followed and any items which are the flip side of your contribution (for example: I listen to his problems. He listens to mine) should be listed across from each other.

Every psychological contract includes at least one and usually several *pivotal* elements—terms which must be met if the relationship is to continue—and many *peripheral* ones—needs and expectations that are desirable but not essential. We will keep up our end of the bargain as long as our pivotal terms are met, even if *none* of our peripheral ones are. For instance, as long as Stephanie's pivotal need—to be appreciated and viewed as indispensable—was met, she would continue to give 110 percent to the import company, even though her peripheral needs—to work reasonable hours, advance further up the corporate ladder, and be paid better—remained unfulfilled.

Go back over both your give and get lists and prioritize each item. Using the first narrow column (labeled MY PRIORITIES), write the letter A beside any items that you consider essential (expectations that must be met if you are to continue this relationship). Use the letter B to denote items that are important but not essential, ones that make the relationship satisfying but which you could do without and might willingly sacrifice in order to keep an A item. C items are those which are least important to you (and you might even be glad to give up).

Then put yourself in the other party's shoes, prioritizing the items according to what you believe he/she/they consider essential (AA), important (BB), or expendable (CC). Use the second narrow column to do this (labeling it THEIR PRIORITIES).

Reciprocity—I'll Meet Your Needs If You'll Meet Mine

The cornerstone of every psychological contract is the principle of *reciprocity*. Each party to the relationship expects to give something in order to get something in return; to meet the other's needs in exchange for having their needs met. Yet, only a relatively small number of these needs and expectations are actually acknowledged and discussed. If they are, the psychological contract is *negotiated* until we reach a mutual agreement on terms we are consciously aware of—the wages and benefits of your job, for example, or the household chores a young child must perform in order to receive his allowance, a teenager's curfew and so on.

More often, there is an *implied* agreement. What we expect from each other and the relationship, although unspoken, is reasonable and likely to be mutually agreed upon because it is sanctioned by society and considered to be the norm in most personal or professional relationships—marital fidelity, for instance, not stealing from an employer, calling in advance for a date, remembering and celebrating birthdays and anniversaries or some variation on the implication that accompanies any partnership based on mutual faith and trust: *"I won't hurt you and you won't hurt me."*

In the third narrow column (labeled TALKED ABOUT), write the letter T beside any item that you and the other participant in the relationship have actually discussed.

In the fourth narrow column (labeled EXPECTATIONS), use an asterisk (*) to denote items which you believe naturally come with the territory of the relationship—anything, whether or not it has been discussed, that anybody in this type of relationship would reasonably expect to give or receive.

Collusion—I'll Hide My True Thoughts and Feelings If You'll Hide Yours

Although it may not have shown up on your worksheet, one of the most common implied terms in any psychological contract involves the unspoken agreement to avoid confronting certain unpleasant issues or expressing certain thoughts or feelings. This is called collusion and it occurs in countless settings.

- "Since no one else is saying anything about this, it must not be as bad or as important as I think it is," the committee members each tell themselves, and assuming that they are making a big deal out of nothing, each keeps quiet.
- "If something could be done about this situation, it would have been done by now," those at the import company rationalized—and found a way to work around Bart. They were in collusion with each other

and with Bart, who got to continue his inappropriate behavior.

- "Everyone else seems to understand what is going on," the students observe and choose not to raise questions that might make them look stupid, while the teacher gets to maintain his illusion that he is a brilliant educator—right up until his students fail the midterm.

- "I know he's wrong, but if I say so he will get angry and reject (fire, yell at, or humiliate) me," we decide. We get to avoid these consequences and he gets to think he is right.

- "I want to be accepted, get promoted, be elected PTA president, get my child into this preschool, or have a good time at this party—and 'going along with the program' is a small price to pay for getting this other thing that I want."

Sounds like the internal messages and motives behind any hidden agenda, right? The twist is that you and the person or people who are involved in an ongoing relationship with you act as if concealing, camouflaging, or misrepresenting certain agenda items is a rule for your relationship that you have both agreed to follow; a condition for being in the relationship at all.

On the back of your worksheet, divide the page into four sections by drawing a vertical line down the middle of the page and a horizontal line across it. Label the top left section "Things I like to reveal/express," the bottom left section "Things I don't like him/her/them to reveal or express," the top right section "Things he/she/they seem to dislike revealing or expressing," and the bottom right section "Things he/she/they act as if they don't like me revealing or expressing." Then fill in each section.

Before moving on, take some time to think about what you and the other party do instead *of confronting unpleasant issues or expressing taboo thoughts and feelings. Where has collusion gotten you?*

Collusion has numerous negative side effects, including perpetuating conditions that are adversely affecting you. It frequently results in a *shared hidden agenda* like the one the import company staff maintained when they griped about Bart among themselves but chose not to rock the boat by mentioning their concerns to anyone who could actually do something about them. Or instead of expressing your true thoughts and feelings, you may make deceptive or manipulative moves and countermoves. They do A and you do B. They say "X" and you say "Z." Before you know it, your entire relationship or the most important interactions between yourself and others are governed by the unacknowledged and often unconscious back-and-forth maneuvering you engage in over and over again. You have unwittingly gotten locked into a rigid and predictable relationship pattern.

Relationship Patterns

Carol and Jeff's relationship resembled a yo-yo. When Carol gave any indication that she wanted to get closer to Jeff, he immediately did something that pushed her away. Then, once she had moved a bit too far away, he did something to reel her back in. His typical response (creating distance) to her agenda (wanting more closeness) triggered her characteristic response (giving him what she assumed he wanted). Her response, in turn, brought to the surface his need for closeness which he fulfilled by subtly letting Carol know that he once again wanted to spend more time with her.

Neither Carol nor Jeff ever talked about their wishes and fears. Indeed, Jeff was not even aware of his. Instead they automatically reacted to the signals they picked up from each other or from their own psyches. Their relationship was defined and in fact controlled by its repetitive pattern of moves and countermoves, a pattern that I call "Don't Cross that Line or Else."

Kate and Michael's relationship also revolved around a predictable stimulus-response pattern, a psychological version of Hide and Go Seek. When she let him know that she was upset but not what was upsetting her, Michael would immediately begin looking for the problem she had hidden. Kate would give Michael hints to let him know if he was "hot" or "cold" (close to or miles away from meeting her needs), and he would keep looking until he stumbled upon the source of her discontent or somehow managed to give her what she wanted all along.

In this instance, Kate's typical behavior (withdrawing and sulking to signal that she was upset) hooked into an assumption found in Michael's agenda (that he was supposed to solve problems by bringing them out into the open). In order to meet this expectation, Michael did precisely what Kate needed him to do (take the initiative to find out and fix what was ailing her) as well as kept the pattern going—even though, by his own admission, it was driving him crazy.

Likewise, Barry and Eddie's diametrically opposed agendas kept them at odds, but also tied into one another in a pattern that looked like an adult version of the child's game Mother May I? Hoping to finagle Eddie into being more cooperative, Barry made tentative moves in that direction. Determined not to cooperate with someone he needed to view as unfair and incompetent, each time Barry took so much as a baby step toward him, Eddie exploded, sending Barry back to square one. Barry would try again. Eddie would send him back again and so on, ad infinitum.

Here are some additional examples that may sound uncomfortably familiar. To make them more readable I have conjured up a twosome and named them Joe and Pamela. In each example, they could be spouses, lovers, friends, a parent and a child, colleagues, siblings, or a boss and an employee. Behavior engaged in by the female player could be as easily engaged in by the male and vice versa.

Village Idiot. Joe asks Pamela to call the theater box office and order tickets to an upcoming show. An hour after she agrees to do this, Pamela phones Joe. "I don't know the box-office phone number," she says. He looks it up for her. Fifteen minutes later she calls again. "Which show did you say?" she asks. He tells her. This time less than five minutes go by before Pamela calls again. "They have lots of different kinds of seats at different prices," she informs him. "Which do you want?" They discuss the options and come to a decision, but just as she is about to hang up, Pamela comes up with something else she does not know. "How did you want to pay for them?" she asks, and Joe, in exasperation, either decides to call himself or promises himself that the next time he needs something like this done, he will not waste his time by asking Pamela to do it.

That was precisely what Pamela was trying to get Joe to do all along. Whether motivated by a fear of doing the wrong thing, resentment over being asked to do something that Joe could have done himself or the determination not to "take orders" from Joe, playing the village idiot was Pamela's way of getting Joe to stop asking her to do things that she did not want to do. The ploy worked until it dawned on Joe that he was handling everything, and started the ball rolling again by asking Pamela to do something he believed "even an idiot" should be able to do.

Who's the Boss? This pattern is similar to the previous one, only more extreme and more likely to end in an argument. Pamela asks Joe to do the laundry. Joe agrees to do it but "forgets," procrastinates, or bungles the task (by washing whites and colors together, for instance). Pamela ends up doing the laundry herself or doing it over and gets angry at Joe. He can't understand why she is so angry. Calling her crazy, unreasonable, or impossible to please (which may be the case in some relationships), he justifies his sense that he should not have to "take orders" from her. Or Pamela might nag Joe about getting the laundry done, which makes him angry. Naturally, he acts out his anger passive-aggressively (by forgetting, procrastinating, or bungling the task).

Yeah, But. . . . Pamela has a problem. She tells Joe about it and asks for his advice. He makes a suggestion. She responds by saying, "Yeah, but . . ." followed by the reason why that option won't work. Joe suggests something else. Pamela counters with another "Yeah, but . . ." until Joe runs out of suggestions and wonders (sometimes aloud) why Pamela asked for his advice in the first place. The truth is that Pamela never really wanted Joe to give her a viable option. What she was unconsciously looking for was confirmation of her belief that the situation was hopeless and that she was not obligated to do anything about it. By offering her alternatives which she could reject, Joe enabled Pamela to fulfill her agenda while reinforcing his perception of himself as a helpful person and his sense that he is superior to Pamela.

You Decide. Pamela asks Joe where he wants to go for lunch, who he thinks is the best candidate for a vacant position in his department, what he wants for his birthday, or to give her his input on a decision that will affect both of them. Joe invariably replies, "I don't know," or "It doesn't make any difference to me," or "I trust your judgment," and tells her to decide. Regardless of the decision that Pamela makes, Joe complains about it or in some way lets her know that it was not the choice he would have made. This is, of course, precisely the reason Pamela asked for Joe's opinion in the first place and why she will continue to ask, even though he will continue to reply, "You decide."

All Better. Joe says, "I'm upset," or "I feel yucky," or seems on the verge of doing something Pamela thinks he will regret. He is not hiding anything from her and would elaborate on his feelings if she gave him a chance to. But she immediately does or says something that she thinks will make Joe feel "all better" or points out the misstep he is about to take. Joe either lets her do this and absolves himself of all responsibility for handling his own problems; lets Pamela know that everything is not all better so that she automatically tries another potential panacea; or gets angry at her for meddling and she sulks or gets indignant, saying, "But I was only trying to help."

Getting Even. In this pattern, both players have the same characteristic response, so it is impossible to say who makes the first move. Joe does something that hurts, embarrasses, or offends Pamela, who gets even at the next available opportunity. Joe then evens the score, which naturally prompts Pamela to retaliate once more. The moves and countermoves continue until they have a "monster" argument that temporarily clears the air or one of them calls a truce by doing something nice for the other.

Injustice Collecting. Instead of getting even at the first opportunity, Pamela, over an extended period of time, collects enough evidence against Joe for her to justify throwing a tantrum or instigating an argument. Joe commits a series of small "sins" which Pamela ostensibly lets slide. Only, in reality, she has neither forgiven nor forgotten. When she has collected a sufficient number of injustices and Joe once again messes up in some relatively innocuous way, Pamela "freaks out," irately blasting Joe for that transgression *and* all the ones she had not commented on previously. Her extreme reaction seems off the wall to Joe. What's more, she pinpoints no one behavior for him to change but rather goes on about two dozen things he believes she would have mentioned before if they really bothered her. Consequently, he does not take her seriously and goes right on doing what he had always done. And so does she.

Dodge Ball. Joe messes up repeatedly, doing things that he in retrospect realizes must bother Pamela or things that she has specifically asked him not to do. Realizing that he will have to pay the piper eventually, as soon as he notices the slightest sign of irritation on Pamela's part (or simply feels guilty enough about his behavior), he does something to please or appease Pamela. If Pamela is easily taken in, she forgets the transgressions and reminds herself that Joe is sweet and considerate. Even if she is not so naive, she is likely to convince herself that Joe knows that he messed up and is letting her know that he won't mess up again. But, of course, he does and then dodges her truly justified reaction once again.

Naturally, all relationships do not include these or any other repetitive pattern of moves and countermoves. But many do and all have the potential to.

Flexibility—No Contract Is Etched in Stone

Many of your expectations and especially the implied terms of your psychological contract predate the relationship itself. For instance, long before you get married, you have ideas about what marriage in general is supposed to be like and how you want your marriage in particular to be. Likewise, you set certain professional goals for yourself prior to entering the work force or hold certain preconceived notions about what it means to work in the catering, publishing, or banking business—even though you have never actually worked in them. In addition, you may associate certain needs and wish-fulfilling responsibilities with certain roles—assuming that bosses should appreciate the work you do, husbands are supposed to take care of you, wives ought to be support- ive, friends have to be on your side no matter what, children must respect you and so on.

To further complicate matters, at the outset of any rela- tionship, most of us *idealize* other people, groups, or compa- nies. We perceive them to be better or at least more like we wish they were than the way they actually are. Any flaws we happen to spot are quickly overshadowed by the positive attributes that dazzle and elate us. For example, under the influence of our individual agendas, we conclude that the organization that just hired us will provide all the job secu- rity, room for advancement, or outlets for creativity that we desire. We decide that a new lover has every quality we have always wanted in a mate. Our new friends seem to have the exact same values, sense of humor, and general outlook on life that we do. And of course, our children are perfect in every imaginable way.

Regrettably, real people and real relationships rarely if ever measure up to our grand illusions. But luckily, our psy- chological contracts are not etched in granite. They are sub- ject to change and can be modified both to account for the expectations that no living, breathing human being could meet, and to adapt to the changing circumstances in our lives, such as getting married, having children, taking a new posi- tion in the same company, and so on.

In the fifth column of your worksheet (labeled CHANGES), for any items that have changed over the course of your relationship, use the > symbol to indicate expecta- tions that are *more* important than they used to be and the < symbol for expectations that are *less* important than they once were.

If you think about the expectations that have changed over the course of your relationship, you may find yourself feeling sad or resentful or recalling the emotional turmoil you went through once it dawned on you that you were not going to have that particular agenda item fulfilled at all or in quite the way you imagined. A psychological contract and a relationship that works for both parties is flexible enough to accommodate both shattered illusions and changing circumstances. However, that flexibility is not easy to come by and most of us at least initially resist altering our expectations in any way. Instead, we become all the more determined to make the other person or the relationship measure up to our standards.

Go back over your lists one last time, circling any items that have been a source of frustration or distress for you or the other party, causing arguments or prompting you to engage in subtle or blatant power plays in order to get your own way. Pay particular attention to those which seem to give rise to ongoing and escalating conflicts, in which case one or both of you may be knowingly or unknowingly *violating the psychological contract.*

Contract Violations

Eight months after he arrived on the scene, Bart made an error too serious to be ignored. He scheduled, but did not show up for, a meeting with Irv, the head of a retail-store chain that did millions of dollars of business with the new-products division.

When Bart finally waltzed in, he was greeted by David and his father, who had managed to avert the crisis. They immediately confronted him with the events that had transpired in his absence. Where had he been, they wanted to know. What explanation did he have for missing such an important meeting?

The real answer to that question was that Bart had scheduled two appointments for the same time and, assuming that Stephanie (who he did not know had called in sick) would handle Irv, he had kept the other appointment—a breakfast meeting with his accountant. Clearly, he could not tell David and his father this and hope to have a job afterward. He lied instead. "I didn't know anything about a meeting," he claimed. "Stephanie must have arranged it and forgot to tell me."

David immediately phoned and chewed out Stephanie, who was stunned. *How dare Bart blame his mistake on me?* she thought. *How dare he make me look bad and, after all the years I'd worked for him and everything I'd done for him, how could David believe Bart?* "If I hadn't been so sick, I think we would have had it out right then and there," she said, "but I just didn't have the energy to fight. So I said, 'If you honestly believe that I did what Bart said I did, then I think you should fire me right now.'"

David did not fire Stephanie and the incident was never mentioned again. Yet, even though unacknowledged, it marked the beginning of the end for this threesome.

You see, when Bart saved his hide by blaming his mistake on Stephanie and making her look bad, he violated their psychological contract. He fulfilled *his* agenda—including his need not to be held accountable for his actions—at Stephanie's expense, making it impossible for her to fulfill *her* agenda—especially her powerful need to be viewed as capable and indispensable (in other words, to look good).

Your psychological contract is violated whenever the person, group, or organization with whom you have a relationship does something that you believe they have agreed not to do or does not do something you expect them to do. Your boss might chew you out in front of your coworkers, for instance. Or your spouse might buy a car without consulting you. Or a company might try to cut its budget by offering wage increases that do not keep up with others in the industry. In one way or another they are keeping you from fulfilling your agenda, and worse yet, they are thwarting a need that you expected and depended upon them to meet.

You can spot contract violations quite easily because they make you feel betrayed, furious, and frustrated. They hurt you, disappoint you, leave you wondering if *anything* about the other person or your relationship will ever live up to your expectations again. They sap your energy and make it difficult or painful to give anything back to the person or organization that is not giving you what you hoped for in return. As Stephanie was, you may be tempted to end the relationship altogether and will sometimes do so on the spot. Or you may dedicate yourself to making the other party live up to your expectations, maneuvering and manipulating in order to get things back to the way they used to be or rewriting the contract so that you are never hurt or disappointed in that way again. Because this move on your part may keep others from meeting their needs, what were once compatible agendas are now set on a collision course, which was precisely what happened to David, Bart, and Stephanie's agendas.

Stephanie, determined never again to let Bart make her look bad, began putting everything she did into writing and circulating memos each and every time she handled one of Bart's responsibilities. Since the information he routinely claimed not to have was down in black and white for all to see, Bart's village idiot act lost its impact, making it more and more difficult for him to get away with not doing his job. In addition, with each new memo the evidence of Bart's incompetence and irresponsibility mounted, making it more and more difficult for David to conceal that he had been wrong to hire him in the first place. Still hell-bent on maintaining the cover-up, David buried his head deeper in the sand, spending most of each work day in his office with the door closed. He barely noticed and rarely complimented his staff. This lack of recognition took its toll on everyone, with Stephanie, who thrived on it, being hardest hit. Already irritable, short-tempered, and plagued by migraine headaches from the stress of handling Bart's job in addition to her own, Stephanie, who felt that "I was killing myself for the good of the company and nobody gave a damn," became less and less willing to solve every little problem that cropped up—and those little problems snowballed into bigger ones that put the entire division in jeopardy. A situation that was once glued together by collusion began falling apart at the seams because of constant conflict.

The Nature of Conflict

Conjuring up images of bitter arguments, ruined friendships, name calling, fist-pounding confrontations, and tension so thick you could cut it with a knife, the word "conflict" makes many of us cringe and cower in fear. Indeed, most of us avoid conflict like the plague—an understandable reaction, considering the messes we have made or watched others make while attempting to resolve them. More often than not, we regress to childish pig-headedness, using any available means to get our needs met—no matter what it costs us, the other person, or our relationship.

At any age and under any circumstances we take on the characteristics of two preschoolers who both have their hearts set on riding a tricycle during recess. They both arrive at the bike shed and discover that there is only one tricycle in it. At that point, they also know that if one of them gets what he wants, it will be impossible for the other to get what he wants —and that is the bare-bones definition of conflict.

Now, suppose that the physically stronger child wrestles the tricycle away from the weaker one; or that the more passive child, assuming that he does not stand a chance of convincing the other child to let him ride the tricycle, automatically gives in and goes off in the corner to sulk. These youngsters would have used a *win-lose* approach to conflict resolution; an approach that involves consciously or unconsciously fulfilling our wishes at someone else's expense and generally leaves a trail of resentment and frustration in its wake. In addition, as you could see from Bart and Stephanie's agenda conflict, the winner's victory is usually short-lived. The loser keeps score and tries harder to win the next time the two do not see eye to eye, to get her needs met in spite of him or make sure he never wins again—which brings us to the second approach to conflict resolution.

This time suppose that one of the two preschoolers unscrews the handlebars and hides them or that one child appears to give up his option to ride the bike, but quickly rushes out of the bike shed, shuts the door, and locks it. Neither child gets to fulfill his wish—the inevitable outcome of a *lose-lose* approach to conflict resolution which is based on the premise that "If I can't win, I'll make sure you don't win either." The futility of such an approach is obvious in the two kids–one tricycle example. Yet, grownups use it on a regular basis—giving in to our spouse on one issue but making him or her miserable by sulking, making cutting remarks, or withholding sex; getting so angry while discussing where to go to dinner or what movie to see that we end up eating leftovers and watching TV; or devoting so much time during a board meeting to bickering about who is to blame for a problem that we never get around to solving it.

Of course, the two youngsters also could have found a way for both of them to ride the tricycle at the same time or agreed on a plan to take turns riding it or struck a bargain so that one child would give up the bike in exchange for being able to use the other's crayons later in the day. In this case, they would have negotiated a *win-win* resolution to their conflict. Each one would have gotten something that they wanted even though it might not have been all that they wanted or necessarily what they set out to obtain. This approach is the one that causes the least damage to us and our relationships and is the most likely to actually solve a problem once and for all. It is also the one that we are least likely to use—and our individual hidden agendas are often to blame.

Returning for the last time to the preschooler example, consider the possibility that these youngsters' conflict over the tricycle was not *just* about who would ride it. What if one child was jealous of the attention the teacher showed the other? Chances are the child would be more interested in winning (or not letting the other child win) than in fulfilling his immediate desire to ride the tricycle.

This principle applies to all of us. If the true nature or source of a conflict is hidden, we will go round after round in the boxing ring. We duke it out, trying time and again to live up to, or get the other party to live up to, the terms of the original agreement—*often without fully understanding what we are doing or what that agreement was.*

Unconscious Expectations and Assumed Agreement

Although you have just learned a great deal about the *conscious* elements of your psychological contract, and even though these new insights are unquestionably beneficial and can positively influence the choices you make during your day-to-day interactions, they only scratch the surface of what actually goes on in any relationship. The fact of the matter is that all psychological contracts are primarily *unconscious.* Indeed, most relationships are held together by *invisible* connections that enable both parties to meet pivotal needs that they do not even know they have.

The unconscious elements of our psychological contracts are by far the greatest in number and often the most important to us. Although they are always unspecified and frequently unrealistic or unattainable, we nonetheless expect those unacknowledged needs, wants, and wishes to be fulfilled. We act as if others should know *what* we need from them and exactly *how* to meet those needs. And we assume that, simply by entering the relationship, they have agreed to live up to those expectations. They, of course, assume the same of us.

What are some of those assumptions? That the other participant in the relationship will:

- agree with your point of view, at least in public and preferably at all times;
- know when something is bothering you and how to make you feel better (and of course, do that without being asked);
- smooth things over, or cover for you so you can go about the "more important" things;
- accept you the way that you are (often translated to mean never criticize or try to change you);
- suppress angry feelings;
- never embarrass you;
- make you, your family, the job, etc., top priority in his or her life.

Other assumed and presumed-to-be-agreed-upon terms involve *double binds* ("Be honest with me, but don't tell me things I don't want to hear"). In other instances, expectations themselves are out in the open and ostensibly agreed upon, but each party has very different ideas about *how* those expectations should be met.

For instance, your employer may think that by singing your praises in staff meetings, changing your job title every six months and giving you a large year-end bonus, he is living up to the implicit terms of a psychological contract that involves recognizing a job well done and showing appreciation for your contributions to the organization. However, because he has yet to raise your base salary in keeping with what others in the industry make, you do not feel recognized or appreciated at all. The consequences of having dissimilar definitions of the same expectation can be devastating—which was certainly the case for one couple I treated.

"He never talks to me," Helen claimed. She and her husband Dan had been married for less than two years when they found themselves in my office. "I *do* talk to her," Dan insisted.

"You don't," she retorted. "Not about anything that matters, anyway."

"That's because the only thing that matters to you is picking our marriage apart," he grumbled. "And I just don't see the point. We wouldn't even be here if you weren't harping on me to talk about us all the time."

In a matter of moments, Helen and Dan were flinging angry accusations at each other. Listening to their indictments of each other, it quickly became apparent that the real culprit was their assumptions about how to make a marriage work.

You see, Dan believed that couples discussed their feelings and the state of their relationship only when a major problem arose. He assumed that the best way to maintain a good relationship was to "leave well enough alone"—which is what he generally tried to do and expected Helen to do as well. However, Helen believed that couples preserved their relationship by talking about it. In her mind, it was absolutely essential for her and Dan to discuss their feelings about each other and the relationship even when no problems existed between them. Included in her unconscious psychological contract was the assumption that—"When I want to discuss the state of our relationship, you will too."

Consciously unaware of their own expectations and completely in the dark about each other's, Helen automatically and repeatedly tried to get Dan to live up to his end of the bargain (and talk about the relationship) while Dan automatically and repeatedly tried to make Helen leave well enough alone (and *not* talk about the relationship).

Their unconscious expectations were like unseen wires connected to bombs in a well-camouflaged mine field. They did not know where they were until *after* they tripped them and set off explosions that shocked, frightened, outraged, and injured them. If you:

- have the same arguments over and over again;
- notice tension remaining in the air after arguments have ostensibly ended;
- watch "little discussions" mushroom into full-scale battles;
- hit and run, bringing up certain topics when the other person has neither the time nor the energy to discuss them;
- have pet peeves and find that certain statements or mannerisms drive you up a wall;
- pick fights with one person after being thwarted in some way by another;

then the unseen forces in your relationship may—in spite of your best efforts—be engineering its demise.

What Happened to David,
Bart, and Stephanie?

As you might expect, Stephanie, who was giving the most and getting the least from the exploitative psychological contract that governed her work relationships, crumbled first. She began to have panic attacks and because of them came to me for psychotherapy. As she began to get healthier, she also began to see just how sick the situation at the import company was and decided to have a heart-to-heart talk with David. He, however, had no intention of listening to what she had to say. For more than a year he had dreaded the moment when his mistake would be fully exposed and he would have to risk making another mistake while attempting to fix the first. And as Stephanie calmly took a seat in his office, he still was not ready to give up the fight.

She began her well planned, often-rehearsed speech. He pulled out the "best defense is a good offense" ploy, immediately interrupting her. "Who the hell do you think you are," he shouted. "Who gave you the right to tell me how to run my division. If you want a job here, you'd better do it instead of trying to do mine."

Although during her previous therapy session we had discussed countless reactions David *might* have, this was not one Stephanie had seriously considered: She just couldn't believe he'd go that far. When it sunk in that he *had,* it was the final straw. It did not just violate their psychological contract, it demolished it. Stephanie did what she believed she had to do in order to maintain what little integrity she had left. She resigned on the spot.

Stephanie went on to get her college degree; no longer feels compelled to "take care of everybody all the time"; and is, in fact, involved in an intimate relationship with a man who not only is not a "wounded bird" but actually nurtures and is supportive of her. She chose *not* to go on doing what she had always done. And as a result, her life and relationships are *not* the way they had always been. They are better.

On the other hand, one month after Stephanie resigned, David's father insisted that David fire Bart, whose incompetence became glaringly obvious after Stephanie's departure. David carried out his father's orders, but because he resented them and convinced himself for the umpteenth time that his father would always usurp his authority and make him feel incompetent, he resigned as well.

Two years later, Bart is in another job and has a new "rescuer." His new colleagues are saying the same things about him that his staff at the import company said, and his boss, who has a number of personal problems on *his* mind, is looking the other way, saying, as David once did, "Nothing horrible is happening, so there's really nothing I need to do."

David is once again working for his father's company, still feeling as if his father is looking over his shoulder waiting for him to screw up, and still devoting most of his energy to covering up his mistakes and waiting for problems to disappear rather than confronting them.

Stephanie changed herself and her circumstances. Bart and David did not. Indeed, they would not. They were stuck on auto-pilot, moving through life without conscious awareness and acting out of instinct and habit, rather than making choices that were in their best interest. Are you?

7

Why on Earth Did I Do That?

How to Tell When You Are Reacting to New Situations in the Same Old Ways

Let me take you on a quick tour of one aspect of the human mind.

Consciousness

All of your thoughts, feelings, memories, and impressions reside in three overlapping compartments,—the *conscious, preconscious,* and *unconscious.* All three of these levels of consciousness operate at all times. One may predominate at a given time, and which one that is fluctuates, depending on the situation, your personality, and many other factors.

The Conscious Mind

Your conscious mind is like a temporary holding cell—containing the immediate reflection of everything you are aware of *at a given moment in time.* Comprised of the sum total of any information your senses are picking up from the environment and whatever you are remembering from the past, your conscious ideas, emotions, memories, and observations change constantly in response to what is going on around you.

According to psychologist William James, being conscious enables us to select what is relevant; choose from among different courses of action; make decisions; and plan ahead. Many of these functions can be seen in the conscious thought process Sara went through during the seconds immediately preceding the confrontation with her mother, Jane. Her conscious thoughts included:

- My mother is walking over to the oven. [a direct observation]
- She is checking the temperature dial to see if I used the right setting. [observation and interpretation]
- Did I? Yes, I'm sure I did. [short-term memory]
- The last time she was here, I burned dinner. I wonder if she remembers. Of course she does. She never forgets anything I do wrong. [a series of memories and conclusions based on past experiences]
- My stomach is in knots. [observation/feeling]
- She's going to say something I won't like. [prediction based on past experience]
- But, I'm not going to let her get to me. [decision/plan]

Although this may seem like a lot for Sara to have going through her mind in a split second, it is minuscule in comparison to everything she could have been consciously aware of at that moment. She did not notice the time, for example, or think about the fact that her daughter would soon awaken from her nap. She did not pay attention to the sound of the lawn mower her husband was riding past the open kitchen window. Nor did she call up memories of dinners that had not burned and that evoked compliments from her mother.

Why? Because our conscious minds have a limited capacity. You can only be aware of so much at one time. As a result, a good deal of what goes on around you does not get noticed at all. It is instantaneously deemed irrelevant and filtered out of your awareness. Although what is or is not admitted to your conscious mind makes a difference in how you perceive and respond to various situations, this limited capacity is necessary and useful, for without that filtering mechanism, you would be overwhelmed and incapacitated by incoming stimuli. Similarly, your memories of every past experience (including what you learned from those experiences and how you feel about them) do not constantly float around in your conscious mind. They are stored elsewhere.

The Preconscious

Melanie, a sociologist, was working on a research project with five other sociologists. They had gotten behind schedule, and so decided to spend several Saturdays collating data at the home of the project director—a man fifteen years Melanie's senior and whom she greatly admired. On the first of these Saturdays, Melanie arrived at the director's home before the other members of the team.

"As soon as I walked in the door," she recalled, "I began to feel strange. I was very jumpy and I had no idea why. Out of the blue, I started babbling about my husband and my kids. It was like I was trying to make sure Bob knew I was happily married, even though he already knew that. I wouldn't sit down, but kept moving around the room, looking at books and knickknacks. If Bob came over to explain something, I immediately moved to a different part of the room. Finally, one of the other researchers arrived and I remember thinking 'Oh, good. Now I'm safe.' "

At the time, Melanie had no idea why she was being plagued by "strange" feelings and behaving in what was, for her, a very strange manner. But later, while describing the incident to her husband, Melanie remembered that while in graduate school more than a decade earlier she had been in a similar situation with one of her professors, who had invited her to his home to complete a journal article they were co-authoring and then made a pass at her. Although her rejection of his sexual overture had been tactful and appropriate, the professor decided not to hire her to assist him on his summer research project—which meant that Melanie had to, at the last minute, look for another summer job as well as lose the extra college credits she would have received.

Clearly, Melanie's baffling behavior in Bob's presence was triggered by the similarities between that situation and the earlier incident, which had unpleasant and unexpected consequences. She was responding to data stored in her *preconscious* mind.

The preconscious is the reservoir of everything you can remember and have access to through voluntary recall—everything that has ever happened to you, everything you have ever thought, felt, or done, and everything you have come to believe or expect which you can bring into your conscious mind at will. In a sense, the preconscious is like an internal hidden agenda. You are not always consciously aware of what is going on at this level of your psyche, but the information would be available to you if you chose to reveal it to yourself by retrieving it from your memory.

Although some of the material stored in your preconscious is upsetting, none of it is shocking enough to be blocked from your conscious mind completely. There is nothing there that you do not already know about. However, at times you lose touch with that information. You may, for instance, pick up the telephone and go to dial a number that you have dialed countless times before, but temporarily be unable to remember it. You may be discussing a client of long standing and for some odd reason be unable to recall his name, or you may have to go back and check to see that you unplugged the iron, because try as you might, you just cannot visualize yourself doing it earlier.

Information stored in the preconscious can and often does influence what you think, feel, or do in the present. Sometimes this old material moves from the preconscious into the conscious—as it did when Sara remembered that she had burned dinner during her mother's last visit. However, you can also be affected by preconscious information *without* being aware of its influence—as Melanie was.

The Unconscious

The unconscious is the domain of thoughts, feelings, and needs that you are completely unaware of having, but which nonetheless influence your life in significant ways. All of your more primitive drives and impulses are stored here: raw feelings like the sense of dread Jenny associated with failing to please or outsmart her father, or the sheer terror you may have experienced each time you were separated from your mother during early childhood; details of various traumas—like a parent's death—that seemed to be more than you could cope with at the time they occurred, as well as any other memories with a powerful emotional charge. Overall, your unconscious is comparable to a lead-lined, triple-locked and booby-trapped file cabinet filled with all of the details of your life that were once too painful, frightening, or incomprehensible to accept—and which you are now unable to remember. As Daniel Goleman, Ph.D., describes in his book *Simple Truths, Vital Lies,* we "forgot" the incident as well as our feelings about it and then "we forgot that we had forgotten it."

As a result, the impulses and memories which we assigned to secret files in the past are unavailable to us at a later date. Unlike material stored in the preconscious, unconscious information cannot be retrieved through voluntary recall. We cannot will ourselves to remember it, although we can gain insights about it with the help of psychotherapeutic techniques like those you have found throughout this book.

However, even though you truly are not aware of it or its influence, unconscious material plays an active role in your conscious thoughts and feelings. You could see this influence clearly in Jenny's predicament. With the exception of the end result—getting off track during her lectures, all of her thoughts, feelings, and decisions occurred at an unconscious level. She unconsciously picked up signals that her audience was losing interest in her presentation, unconsciously remembered what happened when she did not keep her father entertained, and unconsciously linked past to present, interpreting the signals to mean that something terrible was about to happen and her unconscious desire to avoid disaster then compelled her to do something to recapture her audience's attention or win their approval.

All of that happened in the blink of an eye and is a clearcut example of operating on auto-pilot. When a need, fear, wish, or idea about how to handle a situation originates in your unconscious and compels you to behave in a certain way *without* making a stop at the conscious level of your mind, then you are operating on auto-pilot.

Operating on Auto-pilot

To reiterate what I said in the Introduction, during any given day, most of what we do falls under the heading of automatic behavior. When we go through our daily routines; perform certain aspects of our jobs; address our boss in one tone of voice and our children in another; look for oncoming cars before crossing the street; or otherwise conduct ourselves safely, comfortably, and appropriately in many diverse settings, we do so without much or any conscious thought, indepth analysis, or agonizing over the alternatives available to us. We operate on auto-pilot.

On auto-pilot, you can drive the familiar route to work while so absorbed in other thoughts that you reach your destination "before you know it" and cannot recall any details of the ride itself. On auto-pilot, you can photocopy and collate one hundred multipage reports without really paying attention to the task or insert one page upside down twenty times before you notice your mistake. On the other hand, you can be well aware of *what* you do automatically, but find it virtually impossible to explain *why* or *how* you do it. Without physically demonstrating the action, just try telling someone how to tie shoes, make a bed, close a deal, or do anything else you have done repeatedly over an extended period of time. Or ask yourself why, in spite of the fact that you have done nothing wrong, you get nervous when you see a police car; how you can tell that the man or woman seated across the room is attracted to you; or why you immediately assume that disaster is about to strike each time you hear the words "The boss wants to see you," or "Honey, we have to talk." When you ask yourself why you react this way, your answer is apt to be, "I really don't know." And consciously you don't. You noticed, interpreted, and responded to your circumstances instantaneously, using a process that you truly could not see.

Operating on auto-pilot is not about *what* you say or do, but rather *how* and *why* you say or do things. Remember the example I gave back in the Introduction about your getting home from work feeling tired and frazzled, going to the freezer, taking out the chocolate ice cream, scooping some into a dish and eating it? If you are fully aware of feeling tired and frazzled, realize that eating ice cream is something you sometimes do to comfort or reward yourself when you feel that way, consider what else you could do to meet your needs, and then choose to eat the ice cream, you are in the driver's seat making a conscious decision and are not on auto-pilot. From the moment you walk through the door, you are aware of your behavior and your motives. You know you are eating ice cream, why you are eating ice cream—and you are able to enjoy eating it. On the other hand, if you immediately head for the freezer every day after work or reach for the ice cream whenever you feel tired, frazzled, or emotionally off-balance; if you numbly swallow spoonful after spoonful, barely tasting the ice cream—then you are on auto-pilot, being driven by instinct, habit, or needs that are outside your awareness. After the ice cream is gone, you may hardly remember eating it or have trouble believing that you did. You don't really know what motivated you to eat it and may feel guilty, remorseful, or horrified. Why on earth did I do that, you wonder—a sure sign that you were operating on auto-pilot.

In spite of the bewildering nature of some automatic behavior, being on auto-pilot is neither good nor bad in and of itself. On the plus side, it enables you to absorb information from the environment, run it through your memory bank and act in a familiar and comfortable way. The entire process takes a split second and, in many instances, works to your benefit. However, as was apparent in all the examples you found in this book, automatically reacting in your characteristic manner *does not work for you in every situation.*

As I tell my patients, the best way to view your characteristic responses is to recognize that they may not work well in new or baffling situations or when you sense that hidden agendas are involved or feel strong emotions welling up inside you. If you truly care about the outcome of a particular situation or could suffer serious consequences by leaving matters in the hands of fate, then reacting automatically will probably work against you, especially if you continue to respond in your characteristic manner when it is clearly doing you more harm than good.

"Of course I was upset," Kate said indignantly. "Hanging up on me like that was the last thing I expected Michael to do. I never would have treated him so callously. He should have been more sensitive. After all, I wasn't some client or secretary calling about some trivial business problem. I'm his wife and he's supposed to care about me." As you can see, because Michael's actual behavior fell short of Kate's preconceived notion of what he was supposed to do, as far as she was concerned, he had violated their psychological contract. The reality of the situation—that Michael had not known what Kate expected and had treated her forthrightly, not callously—never entered the picture. The moment Michael said "I can't talk now," Kate *was consciously aware of her actions but* not *consciously in control of them.* She was operating on auto-pilot.

First, her thoughts snowballed. "Michael really let me down." Kate sighed. "I remember thinking, how could he do that to me? He's supposed to be on my side." She even entertained the notion that Michael had stopped loving her. "That would explain why he didn't give a damn about what was bothering me," she concluded at the time.

Soon Kate was, by her own admission, "walking around the office like a zombie," and finding it difficult to concentrate while so much of her energy was being used to cope with the nightmarish images she was conjuring up in her mind.

As I listened to Kate recount her distress during an individual therapy session, it occurred to me that there were many things she could have done to help herself feel better right after her conversation with Michael or later that evening. For instance, she could have called Michael back immediately, and by doing so, would have learned that he was indeed in a meeting. When he got home from work, she could have told him that she was angry about his abrupt termination of her call or let him know how upset she had been when she called and why. And even if she had chosen to give him the silent treatment, once he asked what was wrong, she could have told him instead of withdrawing further in hopes of getting her needs met without ever revealing what they were.

However, because instinct and habit were in the driver's seat, none of these options occurred to Kate. She went directly from stimulus to response; from feeling hurt and threatened by Michael's behavior to withdrawing from the source of her frustration and confusion.

As you might expect, Kate reacted in this manner quite regularly, not just with Michael, but also when she disagreed with her coworkers, believed that her boss was not showing enough interest in or appreciation of her work, or felt that she was being taken for granted by her friends. It might take hours, days, or months, but most—although not all—of these people eventually "came around," making an effort to win Kate back even though they usually did not know why they "lost" her in the first place.

While in the self-imposed exile, Kate always felt miserable and terrified that the person from whom she was withdrawing would not be drawn back to her. Indeed, she walked around in a constant state of anxiety, sometimes getting so worked up that she couldn't sleep, eat, concentrate, or get through the day without taking several Valium. In spite of the suffering it caused her, why was Kate's *characteristic response* still her first and, more often than not, her only response to most situations? Because her psyche was "hot-wired" to bypass logic and reason whenever it consciously or unconsciously experienced the slightest twinge of anxiety.

When external circumstances pose a threat to your physical or emotional well-being, you experience *reality anxiety,* or more to the point, fear. Internal forces stir up another kind of anxiety, *anxiety proper*—an unconscious fear of falling apart, losing control, or being overwhelmed by emotions. Anxiety proper may be triggered by:

- Affronts to your self-esteem—anything that suggests you may be less adequate or worthwhile than you perceive yourself to be (being passed over for a promotion and feeling inadequate);
- Powerlessness—the assessment that you are helpless to cope with a situation—for example, natural disasters or the fact that you are aging and can no longer do some of what you used to do when you were younger;
- Fear of rejection or abandonment by almost anyone;
- Loss of emotional support (after moving to a new city; the departure of a respected colleague or supervisor at work; terminating therapy and so on);
- "Dangerous" impulses that are close to breaking through to the conscious level of your psyche (your unacknowledged sexual desire for your best friend's spouse; an unrecognized urge to "decimate" someone by saying or doing something you know will hurt and believe will destroy that person);
- Guilt that occurs when you are consciously aware of

an instinctive wish (for instance, to take a day off just for the heck of it or let the baby cry instead of getting out of bed to feed or change her) that your inner voices tell you is something a "good" person is not supposed to do; or when you actually act on an impulse, doing something that those inner voices "punish" you for by bombarding you with negative judgments and criticism.

In addition, your internal alarm system is almost always tripped when you unconsciously or consciously recognize that a present-day interaction includes people or circumstances that resemble unsettling past experiences which involved rejection, disapproval, loss, humiliation, or other negative consequences.

For instance, Kate's mother, who was prone to extreme mood swings, which I suspect were caused by manic-depressive illness, was an inconsistent parent, to say the least. When she was in a "down" mood, she was attentive to Kate, practically smothering her with affection. Needing nurturing herself, Kate's mother would hug and kiss and hold Kate in her arms for hours. However, when she "switched gears," as Kate put it, she would have no time for Kate at all. Giddy to the point of seeming drunk or frenetically cleaning or talking on the telephone, Kate's mother literally told Kate to get lost and had, on occasion, slapped her daughter or launched into a verbal tirade against her because Kate had inadvertently interrupted something she was doing. Never knowing when her mother's mood would change, Kate was caught off guard each time it did, then felt mortally wounded and wondered if she had done something to warrant her mother's rejection. Over the years she had come to realize that her best bet was "to retreat and wait out the storm." Once her mother "settled down," she "came back" to Kate.

Clearly, withdrawing and distancing herself from the

people she wished to be close to was something that Kate learned at a very young age. However, she also learned when to withdraw—as soon as she picked up the slightest, subtlest sign that she had not received (or would not be receiving) the love and attention she needed and expected (whether or not she had conveyed this need and whether or not the other person was actually withholding).

Under these circumstances, Kate was aware of feeling anxious, and even though she had blown things out of proportion, would generally pinpoint what immediate events had stirred up that feeling. You may be able to do this too. Or you may consciously feel anxious, frightened, guilty, or confused, but have no idea or only a vague notion of what is making you "antsy." Sometimes you will notice no change in your emotional state at all. However, much like a dog whistle that produces a sound only dogs can hear, the unpleasant feelings that escape your conscious awareness are "heard" by your unconscious and perceived as a threat to your physical or psychological survival. In the name of self-preservation, your psyche immediately moves to remove the threat, to reduce anxiety in any way it can.

Whenever circumstances prevent you from going right to the source of your anxiety and eliminating it through some sort of direct action, you find another way to solve the problem and win the battle raging in the recesses of your mind. You perform a psychic magic act so everything stays the way it is but looks and feels okay. The lion's share of your own and other people's most inexplicable and unproductive automatic behavior is the by-product of the *unconscious coping mechanisms* that you use to accomplish this feat.

For instance, both Eddie, the argumentative substance-abuse counselor, and Howard, the entrepreneur who was determined to have "the finer things in life," relied on the unconscious coping mechanism of *projection*. They coped with their own frightening or unacceptable thoughts, feelings, or character traits by attributing them to other people. And Stephanie used the unconscious coping mechanism of *reaction formation*, which transformed a "bad" wish into a "good" one.

As a young girl growing up in a family devoted to the care of her terminally ill younger brother, Stephanie often longed for more nurturing and attention, especially from her mother. But every time she sought to satisfy this need, she, in one way or another, received a message that said, *I cannot take care of you. And since Bobby is very sick and will die without my care, you must not expect me to.* By the time she was three, Stephanie had filed that message in her unconscious, twisting it around a bit so that, at the most fundamental level, she believed *it is wrong to need nurturing and bad to want to be taken care of.* At four, Stephanie discovered a way to identify with and be close to her mother. She helped her mother take care of Bobby, and at five she could do everything from change oxygen tanks to make Bobby's bed while he was lying in it.

As a result, she learned that *it is good to take care of others.* In fact, whenever Stephanie unconsciously felt an urge to be taken care of, she automatically replaced the "bad" wish with the "good" one and was *consciously* aware of wanting to take care of others. The coping mechanism of *reaction formation* was one of the forces that convinced Stephanie as an adult to put other people's needs before her own and, among other things, to sacrifice herself for the good of the import company.

Unconscious coping mechanisms lessen the impact of any trauma, make painful circumstances more tolerable, and maintain equilibrium until a better solution can be found. We all have them, but we do not use them all of the time. After all, we are not anxious about *everything.*

As is true with all automatic behaviors, we rarely realize we are using unconscious coping mechanisms *while* we are using them. When your automatic words or actions end up hurting you, other people, or your relationships, your shock, dismay, and remorse are genuine. You are being honest when you claim, "I never meant to hurt anyone," and if you say, "I have no idea how I got myself into this mess," you are not playing dumb. If you were operating on auto-pilot, you truly were not aware or consciously in control of your thoughts, words, or actions. You could not see (or stop) what was happening while it was happening. However, if you examine your behavior after the fact, you can gain insights (conscious awareness of your unconscious processes and their effect on your life) that can be of enormous value to you in the future.

In the appendix you will find additional information on unconscious coping mechanisms, as well as tips for spotting them in yourself and others. The following exercise can help you to gain insight into the other characteristic responses and auto-pilot behaviors you use in anxiety-provoking situations.

Why on Earth Did I Do That?

The next time you ask yourself, "Why on earth did I do that?" take some time to actually answer—instead of repeating the question until you have worked yourself up into a frenzy or down into a depressed state. Doing your best not to dwell on what you now think you *should* have done (and how stupid you were not to), consider the following:

RECALL EXERCISE 9

What did you do?

Was it a characteristic response?

Think back to the last time that using this maneuver or responding in this manner actually worked for you.

What were the circumstances and what were your thoughts, feelings and goals under those circumstances?

Were there similarities between this old experience and the more recent one which might have triggered your automatic responses? What were those similarities?

What made the more recent experience different from the one in which the same response worked? How might those differences have contributed to the failure of your way of doing things?

Using your 20-20 hindsight, what options can you now see were available to you? Consider what you wish you had done as well as what people whose judgment you trust might have done (ask them if you'd like).

List several possible consequences (both positive and negative) for each of those options and, based on this assessment, identify those which would have been more *helpful than what you actually did.*

For future reference, make a mental note of the information about yourself that you gathered as well as the alternatives you generated by answering these questions. Since acting automatically is a hard habit to break, you may have to do this exercise many times over before you are able to actually catch yourself responding in your characteristic manner.

Getting Locked In on Auto-pilot

"I'm a people person," said Barry (the counseling supervisor who had so much trouble dealing with Eddie, his coworker). "I like people and I have a pretty good understanding of what makes them tick. Or at least I used to think so. Now

. . . well, now, I keep wondering if I was just lucky before. I ran into people like Eddie in the past, but I was always able to get them to work *with* me instead of against me. I thought that was something I was good at, but now I'm not so sure."

Clearly, Barry's baffling interactions with Eddie were beginning to undermine his confidence. Naturally, he did not want Eddie to know that he was feeling threatened and unsure of himself. And so, he automatically kept at least part of his psychological agenda hidden, using a number of different maneuvers to cover up his insecurities, finagle Eddie into being more cooperative and keep his own exasperation at bay. For instance, no matter how hostile or argumentative Eddie became, Barry suppressed his true feelings, maintaining a calm, unruffled exterior. If Eddie began a verbal assault, Barry immediately backed off, telling himself that he would raise the subject again when he came up with the right approach or when Eddie could discuss the matter more rationally. Barry made educated guesses about what was really bugging Eddie, deciding Eddie must be sick of working on the detox unit and offering to transfer him elsewhere. He frequently relied on setups—like asking if a disturbance on the detox unit had prevented Eddie from attending a staff meeting, already knowing that that was not the case. When that didn't work, he tried breaking down Eddie's resistance by asking for his opinion before instituting policy changes and going out of his way to notice and make positive comments about anything Eddie did right.

There was nothing inherently wrong with Barry's approach. The maneuvers he used were neither exploitative nor self-defeating. Indeed, they were appropriate to the situation and had worked to both Barry's and his staff's advantage many times over. They simply *did not work with Eddie,* who because of his own hidden agenda, viewed every move Barry made as either unfair and abusive or a sign of idiocy. Yet

Barry kept plugging away, convinced that if he tried hard enough he would find a way to get through to Eddie.

Although the specific actions Barry took in order to get through to Eddie required a good deal of conscious thought and planning, he was nonetheless pursuing that course of action automatically. First of all, figuring people out and finding the incentive that would make them cooperate was a characteristic response.

"Dealing with people is like putting together a jigsaw puzzle," Barry explained. "You have to find the right pieces and fit them into the right places. If I have a problem with someone, I just ask myself, What piece is missing from the puzzle?, find it, and put the puzzle together again." This rather sophisticated approach—which incorporated all of the maneuvers Barry used on Eddie—was the one Barry typically used to both supervise his staff and get along with people in any setting. Barry was so attached to this way of conducting himself that almost any other approach just didn't feel right to him.

Second, he continued to use the same approach even though it was not working and even though he was suffering as a result of it. For instance, Barry had ample evidence that the rest of the staff respected his authority and appreciated his guidance, but he could not seem to focus on the positive or find the energy to be as involved with them as he used to be. With each passing day, Barry's feelings of self-doubt and inadequacy grew stronger, as did his dissatisfaction with his job —a situation he was thoroughly convinced could be remedied *if and only if* he finally got through to Eddie.

Perhaps you are thinking, "Barry should just give it up already. Eddie's not worth all that aggravation," or "Who needs all this psychological mumbo jumbo. The guy's a jerk. Why doesn't Barry just fire him?" Your point would be well taken, if Barry were consciously controlling his thoughts and actions. But he was not. He switched over to auto-pilot each time Eddie provided the stimulus (being difficult) that set off an alarm in Barry's unconscious. Threatening his self-image and thwarting his expectations, each encounter with Eddie (and soon, merely anticipating the next encounter) activated Barry's early warning system—anxiety. "If you were half the person you think you are, Eddie wouldn't be able to get to you," an inner voice said. "You must get through to him, because that is what a good supervisor is supposed to do." Naturally, Barry responded to this message in his characteristic manner. What's more, each time Barry tried to get through to Eddie and failed, the inner voice got louder and more insistent, compelling Barry to try harder to make his typical approach succeed.

Although Eddie's job was protected by a union—making it difficult for Barry actually to fire him, there were plenty of other avenues Barry could pursue. Most obvious was to follow the established procedures for disciplining employees who do not comply with hospital policies, instead of trying to explain and single-handedly change Eddie's inappropriate behavior.

Barry also could have lessened the impact of his problem with Eddie by paying less attention to it and more attention to the rest of his staff, channeling his energy into the many positive program changes he had planned for. He could even have tried to release some of his frustration through exercise or regained some peace of mind through meditation. Unfortunately, Barry did not consider any of these alternatives. It never even occurred to him to look for other options. He was *locked in* to his typical way of doing things—and you may be too.

When secret keeping and characteristic responses that have worked for us in the past do not achieve their desired goal, they create a curious quirk in our conduct: instead of doing something different, the vast majority of us do the same thing only louder, more desperately, and from an outside observer's perspective, more stubbornly. We hit the same note over and over again, a bit more forcefully each time—as Kate did when simply clamming up did not get Michael's attention. Her next moves were to withdraw physically—by holing up in the bedroom—and then sexually—by pretending to be asleep when Michael came to bed. Similarly, Jenny, who typically did whatever she could to please others and adjusted her own behavior at the slightest sign of disinterest or disapproval, used both responses during one presentation after another until her boss called her into his office to discuss the possibility that she might not be cut out for the line of work she had chosen. And of course, Barry, in a valiant attempt to turn the insubordinate Eddie into a cooperative team player, watched one familiar and previously useful tactic after another backfire, only to become even more determined to get through to Eddie.

When you are locked in on auto-pilot you automatically apply to any confusing, frustrating, or anxiety-provoking situation the solution that is most familiar and comfortable, and which allowed you to protect yourself in the past. And each time you take that particular path, it becomes more and more difficult to choose a different route. Eventually, like Barry, you get trapped in a vicious cycle—automatically responding in your characteristic manner to others who are apt to be acting and reacting in their characteristic manner as well.

The cycle can go on forever. *But it does not have to.* You can get off auto-pilot and even in the most baffling situations make conscious choices that are in your best interest.

8

Getting off Auto-pilot

Learning to Steer
Your Own Course

- "It's hopeless. I've tried every trick in the book, but nothing works."
- "Sure I could change, but what good would that do me? This would still be a rotten place to work."
- "Why should I be the one to change? *He's* making *me* miserable."
- "It's really not that bad. Other people have it worse."

Those are the sounds of foot dragging, stonewalling, hedging one's bets, procrastinating, and just plain resisting change. You make them when you realize that you are going to remain stuck in your dead-end job, unsatisfying relationship, or some other self-defeating situation unless you try a new approach. Still, you make at least one last-ditch effort *not* to do anything differently than you have in the past. Like children ordered to clean their rooms or eat their vegetables, you whine "Do I *have* to?"

Do I *Have* To?

Of course, the truth is that you do *not* have to change. What you do with the information and insight you have accumulated is up to you. It is your choice. You can choose to change something that you do not like about yourself or your circumstances (yelling at bank tellers and grocery store clerks because you are angry at your boss; smoking cigarettes when you feel upset; picking up the slack for an incompetent coworker). Or you can choose not to. You can choose to change something that you *do* like but which is nonetheless getting in your way (buying clothes with money you could be saving to buy a house; gossiping—which your boss seems to think makes you untrustworthy and thus unpromotable; saying exactly what's on your mind to people who are put off by your openness). Or you can choose not to.

You can opt to *behave* differently even though your feelings remain the same. For instance, you might spend less time listening to your parents complain about their health and your siblings, even though you feel guilty about it. Or you can decide to keep your behavior and change your attitude. You might, for example, spend as much time with your parents as you always have, but accept rather than resent the fact that they dump their complaints on you. Or you might continue to work overtime not because you feel guilty about leaving a task unfinished or are trying to avoid going home to an empty apartment, but because of the pleasure and sense of accomplishment completing a task gives you. You can set goals for yourself and start moving toward them or consciously choose to keep the life you have and start enjoying it.

However, clinging more tightly than ever to your old, familiar habits even though they are hurting you, giving up your seat in the lifeboat in order to stay on the deck of the *Titanic* even though you know it is sinking, is *not* a conscious choice. It is a reflex action; an automatic response to an almost overwhelming and largely unconscious urge to dig in your heels and stay where you are—no matter what it costs you.

All Revved Up, But Going Nowhere

Have you ever spent the night preceding an unfamiliar or unsettling experience, such as leaving for college or starting a new job, having one disturbing dream after another? Those dreams were your psyche's way of screaming "Don't do it!" even though, on a conscious level, you were relatively certain that what you were about to do was not going to hurt you. Programmed for self-preservation and primed to maintain the status quo, your unconscious mind interprets almost any change in your typical behavior patterns as a potential threat to your well-being. Faced with this disruption in your usual, albeit unproductive routine, it is not about to abandon its first line of defense—the characteristic responses and other habits it has been automatically activating for a long, long time. In fact, in addition to sending warnings to you in your sleep, any time that you are about to take a significant step in a new direction, your psyche flips one switch after another so that "Don't change anything" reverberates through your unconscious and you cannot help but respond to it or to the conscious fears that plague you.

Whether you are considering the possibility of asserting yourself instead of slacking off when you feel unappreciated at work, or expressing your feelings instead of drowning them in a fifth of whisky or a pint of fudge ripple ice cream—the first thoughts that come time to mind are bound to be negative ones.

You ponder the horrible fates that could befall you. You home in on everything you stand to lose. When conjuring up worst-case scenarios, in no time flat you can go from worrying about asking for a raise to envisioning yourself being fired, penniless and sleeping on steam vents with all your worldly possessions crammed into shopping bags. While you may be able to laugh at so preposterous an image, the less tangible losses you anticipate can rarely be sloughed off so easily.

Your life as is may not be terrific, but it is familiar and predictable. If you changed any aspect of it, you might lose that sense of safety and security and never find it again. You might lose the competitive edge that your abrasive demeanor and power plays provide. You might have to remove the character armor that conceals the flaws you believe will be your undoing or give up the comfortable numbness that keeping secrets from yourself and operating on auto-pilot creates. Would you really be able to survive without your hidden agendas and characteristic responses?

What if, by starting to peel away old layers of self-protection, you uncover a deep, dark, life-threatening secret? Would you fall apart at the seams? What if you exhume old memories or face present-day realities and feel horrible pain? What if the pain never ends? By being more open and forthright than you have been in the past, aren't you making yourself vulnerable to yet more pain? And if you change yourself or your circumstances, couldn't you make matters worse instead of better?

With so much at stake, is it any wonder that paralysis sets in when the time comes for us to put our money where our mouths are? Who can blame us for wanting to wait for time to heal all that ails us, to change our unconscious for us and reveal the perfect, preferably painless solution to our problems? Unfortunately, while we are waiting around to be miraculously rescued from our banal or even painfully demeaning existences, time marches on, taking countless opportunities and most of life's potential pleasures with it.

When you resist change, you are like a car stuck in neutral with its engine racing. Burning fuel and spinning your wheels, you bounce back and forth between identifying what you need to do and talking yourself out of doing it, arming yourself with insight and options then disarming yourself by coming up with reasons not to use them. You get all revved up but do not move an inch in any direction.

Yet ironically, the fears that paralyze you may have little or no basis in reality. The disastrous outcomes and horrendous consequences you envision are *not* happening. Of course, they might happen. But then again, they might not. The present-day events that *feel like* unsettling past experiences are not really the same as those old incidents and are not predestined to turn out the same unsatisfying way they once did. You are watching a scary movie and being frightened by the fake blood and special effects. It seems real and you act as if it is when you could simply change channels and view your circumstances in a different and decidedly more positive light.

Changing Channels—How to Develop a More Positive Mindset

Being scared is not a good enough reason not to try a new approach. Giving in to your fears and permitting unconscious forces to call the shots for you is what you have unwittingly been doing for years. And where has that gotten you, except more deeply mired in the baffling situations and bewildering relationships that you picked up this book in hopes of unraveling? If you are ever to solve the mysteries of your everyday life and extract yourself from the tangled web of hidden-agenda interactions, you must drum up the courage to overcome the fears that are fueling your resistance to change. Although I cannot supply it for you, I can offer you the mainstays of a positive mindset that make it easier to find that courage within yourself.

Read the following statements carefully, allowing them to sink in and take root in your mind. They are positive thoughts that are, no doubt, more accurate than your negative ones and an energy source rather than an energy drain.

1. "No matter where I am right now and how bleak things seem right now, I did not get here because I was stupid, crazy, or inept. I did what I had to do to get vital needs met; what I learned to do to survive. Whether or not it is working in my best interest right now, the coping style I adopted was *ingenious and effective* given the limitations I had at the time."

2. "I have fewer limitations and more alternatives now. I am not six years old or eight or sixteen, and the incidents that occurred when I was younger are not happening now. I am an adult with more know-how and resources at my command. Because of this I can handle the problems I encounter today differently and with more conscious awareness."

3. "No feeling, be it fear, anxiety, pain, or sadness, is ever as unmanageable or devastating as I imagine it will be. Emotions, no matter how distressing or disheartening, do not last forever. They may not go away as quickly as I wish they would. They may re-

emerge periodically. But they do lessen in intensity and stay for shorter visits each time they return."

4. "No one changes perfectly—or overnight. I may wish that I could jettison everything, discard all of my unproductive habits at once and be guaranteed that I will *never* be that way again, but that is not going to happen. Since aiming for all or nothing is a prescription for disaster, I will take one step at a time, being gentle with and forgiving myself for the backward steps I will take from time to time."

5. "I cannot and do not have to be aware and in conscious control twenty-four hours a day. I do not constantly have to look at myself under a microscope. If I feel like it and am willing to accept the results I get, I can choose not to think about what is happening and just let it happen."

6. "I am not asking myself to change *everything* about myself. There are countless characteristics, attitudes, and attributes that are fine and working for me just the way they are."

7. "Change is *not* synonymous with loss even though all change involves *some* loss. In fact, I stand to gain:
   • the flexibility to roll with the punches and adjust to unexpected turns of events;
   • freedom from the repetitive patterns that get me into the same sorts of messes over and over again;
   • new coping skills that will make my life less stressful and more manageable;
   • an end to the frenzied pace and anxiety that comes from trying to control things that are beyond my control;
   • the return of emotions like joy, excitement, compassion, and hope, which I buried along with my fear, sadness, and anger;

· the self-esteem that comes along with making decisions for myself."

Positive statements like these counteract the pessimism and fear that undermine your resolve to change. Indeed, they do that so effectively that I recommend making copies of the above list and keeping them with you for future reference. Whenever you are tempted to give in to your fears or give up on yourself, read them again and transform the energy you are expending on excuses or self-recriminations into energy that propels you in any new direction you decide to go.

Naturally, a few affirmative statements and more positive attitudes are not all that you will need to actually get off auto-pilot. An obstacle that can be even more tenacious than your negativity still stands in your way. That obstacle is the anxiety that switches you over to auto-pilot in the first place. To overcome that obstacle, you must reprogram your reaction to the baffling situations of everyday life, replacing the responses you typically use to *control* or *squelch* your anxiety with cognitive maneuvers that allow you to *tolerate* it and take action in spite of it.

Tolerating Anxiety

Our thoughts raise the emotional ante on any already anxiety-provoking situation. By adding more current to circumstances that already carry an emotional charge, we literally make ourselves *more* anxious and ensure that our emotional state would become intolerable, triggering the automatic behavior we want to discontinue. If we are ever to achieve our goals, we have to reverse the process.

Anxiety itself is inescapable. You can absorb volumes of information about human nature, gain virtually limitless insight into your own unconscious processes and learn count-less coping skills, but still encounter circumstances that stir up insecurity and apprehension. Operating with more conscious awareness and making conscious choices that are in your best interest does not prevent you from running into situations that may not turn out the way you want or expect them to. You will still confront potential failure, rejection, embarrass-ment, and other affronts to your self-esteem that your psyche will continue to treat as threats to your survival. And any-thing that resembles an unsettling experience from your past will go right on making your heart race, your head throb, your palms sweat, and your mind reel. Those are the givens of living in an imperfect world. However, your response to anxiety-provoking circumstances is *not* a given, but a variable, something that is within your control and that you *can change* if it gets in your way.

TO REDUCE ANXIETY, LOWER THE STAKES INSTEAD OF RAISING THEM

- I *never* know what to say.
- He *always* does this.
- I'm going to screw this up.
- Why is she doing this *to me?*
- He's not going to like this.
- It will probably be like this for *the rest of my life.*
- What's the matter with me?
- What's the matter with them?
- If he thinks he's going to get away with this, he has another think coming.
- If we aren't going to do it *the right way,* why bother doing it at all?

Each of these ideas and many others like them increase anxiety. How? By convincing you that more is at stake during an interaction than may actually be the case. For instance, thoughts with the words "always" or "never" in them persuade you that isolated incidents are part of a larger and presumably unchangeable pattern. Momentarily at a loss for words, you think, "I never know what to say," churning out a blanket indictment of your communication skills that undermines your self-confidence and makes the situation (which demands communication) seem completely unmanageable. Similarly, assuming that the circumstances you find yourself in today will last *for the rest of your life* and that any decision you make in the present will have an irreversible impact on your future makes a situation or decision seem more risky. You can't drive stakes much higher than believing you will be stuck with something until the day you die.

Predicting failure, or interpreting other people's actions as intentional attempts to hurt, undermine, or humiliate you, naturally prompts you to raise a defensive shield to ward off that threat. Concluding that something is wrong with you or other people, blaming and finding fault leads to guilt and self-punishment or anger and retaliatory actions that may very well be unwarranted. And even when justified, such a perspective consumes psychic energy that could be used far more productively. Your problems do not get solved and you get all the more anxious about them.

Fortunately, your thoughts can lower the stakes as well as raise them. By altering your interpretation of events and interactions, you can reduce anxiety to a level that you can tolerate enough to act in your own best interest. You can reverse the flow of current by *talking back to the anxiety-provoking messages you are sending yourself.*

You must realize that your perception of what is going on around you is a response to feelings, not facts. When you find yourself speechless, you *feel* as if you are completely incapable of communicating and have always been. However, if that feeling were a fact—an accurate representation of reality

—you could prove it. You could honestly say that you had never held a conversation, ordered a meal in a restaurant, answered or asked a question, talked about the Saturday morning cartoons with your six-year-old, or hammered out the details of your wedding plans with your in-laws. Of course you have done these things and will no doubt do some of them again. Consequently, the conclusion that you never know what to say and are a complete washout when it comes to communicating is baloney and you can tell yourself that. You can replace the stakes-raising thought with a more accurate and less anxiety-provoking one: "I sometimes have trouble choosing my words and this seems to be one of those times. That does *not* mean that I won't come up with something to say or stand here like a speechless idiot. I am quite capable of communicating." Then, having lowered the stakes a bit and stopped your anxiety from snowballing, you can begin considering your options (admitting that you don't know quite what to say, asking a question, requesting that the other person repeat or clarify his statement, telling the other person that you need some time to gather your thoughts and so on).

Likewise, if you start thinking, "I'm going to screw this up," you can revise your internal script so that your line reads: "I'm worried about making a mistake, but that does not mean I actually will." You can then check in with yourself to see if your fear is warranted or simply the by-product of something you are remembering, telling yourself, or expecting to happen. If your fear is reality-based, you can take steps not to "screw up" (by obtaining the skill or information you need, asking for assistance, paying added attention to certain details and so on).

Take some time now to try the talk-back approach to reducing anxiety. Using a past or present baffling situation as a frame of reference, jot down your thoughts about that situation, especially those that seem to portray your circumstances as riskier or more hopeless than they may actually be.

Then revise your thoughts to depict reality more accurately, turning "always," "never," or "the rest of my life" into "sometimes," "occasionally," or "at the moment"; countering prophecies of failure with predictions for success; describing what seems to be happening rather than who might be at fault and generally opening doors instead of setting up obstacles.

Reread your statements several times, allowing your revised point of view to sink in and noting any change in your feelings about the baffling situation.

By reframing your perceptions of certain circumstances, they immediately become less frightening, infuriating, or frustrating. You may even begin to see options for dealing with the situation, options that were previously concealed by your hopelessness, indignation, or catastrophizing.

You can also use the talk-back technique on your "old tapes"—the thoughts and feelings left over from past experiences, which reemerge to undermine your confidence and talk you out of trying anything new. You can conduct dialogues with your inner critic, judge, victim, or any other internal voice instead of taking at face value what they have to say about your self-worth. Indeed, consciously countering negative self-talk with new facts and more positive perceptions is something you will want to do on a regular basis, developing a new productive habit, one which will ultimately enable you to live with your anxious feelings when they arise.

THOUGHT STOPPING

Thought stopping is another *cognitive maneuver* that enables you to relieve anxiety by changing your reactions rather than altering the situations that trigger them. It temporarily turns off the part of your brain that is feeding you information you cannot handle and is particularly effective when unwelcome, anxiety-provoking thoughts intrude at inopportune moments, hamper your concentration or interfere with other activities. It is also an alternative to the talk-back technique, which is sometimes too difficult and time-consuming to use while in the midst of a baffling interaction.

Based on the simple and logical principle that none of us can consciously focus on more than one thought at a time, the thought-stopping technique allows you to get rid of unwanted thoughts by saying or thinking *Stop!* or visualizing a stop sign when they come to mind. Here's how to do it:

Focus your attention on a self-defeating or unproductive thought. You can use one of those you identified earlier if you'd like. Once that thought is clearly in your mind, imagine a voice shouting, *Stop!* or say it out loud. Then close your eyes and take a deep breath.

Open your eyes and focus your attention on something else. Take a really good look at your hand, listen to music, do a household chore, or a work-related task, or balance your checkbook. If the negative thought returns, start over, beginning with the word *stop.*

The more you practice this technique, the more adept at it you will become. Whenever you notice that a self-defeating or anxiety-provoking thought has spontaneously appeared in your mind, you can silence it quickly and effectively, sending your anxious feelings packing as well.

CONTROLLING THE SYMPTOMS

You can use your mind to manage your physical reactions to anxiety as well as your emotional and intellectual ones. Doing that is a must for those of you who become so panicky and physically uncomfortable that focusing on and reversing your thought processes is virtually impossible. Of course, it is helpful for others as well. After all, the ultimate antidote to anxiety is relaxation, the ability to slow yourself down and be calm.

Step One:
Conjure Up a Calm Scene.

Sit down and write a short, short story. It should be a story with no plot, no car chases, no surprise endings. All it has to do is describe the most calm, peaceful, relaxing circumstances you can imagine. It should include as many details as possible about where you are and what you are doing (or not doing); the sights, sounds, smells and so on that you are using your senses to experience. Here is an example to guide you while you write your own story or, if you find it appealing, you can adopt it as your calm scene.

> I am floating down a stream in a small boat, lying on my back watching the sunlight sneak through the leaves on the tree branches that seem to be reaching out to touch each other from opposite shores. It is early autumn and those leaves have begun to change colors. The sun warms me and the cool gentle breeze feels like silk brushing my skin. It is very quiet here, so quiet that I can clearly hear rustling leaves and bird songs, ripples in the water and my own breathing. As the stream rocks me slowly like a baby in a cradle, I have nowhere to go, nothing to do and only one thought in my mind—"I am calm and relaxed."

Read the words you have written several times. Then shut your eyes and visualize every detail in your mind, mentally videotaping it for future viewing.

Step Two: Physical Relaxation.

After reading all the way through the following step-by-step relaxation exercise, take some time to try it, scheduling a half dozen ten- to fifteen-minute practice sessions over several days. You might want to tape a record of yourself reading the exercise, then play it back.

1. Get in a comfortable position in a quiet place. Plan ahead so that you will not be interrupted. Take the phone off the hook if you have to.

2. Close your eyes and focus your awareness on your breathing, as if your breath were breathing you. Extraneous thoughts will come to mind. Let them pass through without concentrating on them, gently bringing yourself back to your inhaling and exhaling when you notice your awareness has strayed from your breath. Remember, however you are breathing is just fine.

3. Next, turn your attention to your feet. Tense the muscles in your feet; hold them in a tensed position for a slow count to three, then relax those muscles. Take a moment to notice and appreciate the difference between tension and relaxation.

4. Repeat the tense-hold-relax technique on your lower legs, thighs, buttocks, stomach, back, shoulders, arms, hands, neck and face muscles. Notice the feeling of relaxation that flows throughout your body. If any area still seems tense, repeat the tense-hold-relax process on it.

5. After several minutes of sheer pleasure and serenity, once again focus on your breathing and then, when you are ready, open your eyes. Sit quietly for a few moments before getting up and resuming other activities.

This relaxation technique and countless others not only reduce muscle tension that results from stress and anxiety but also reenergize you, leaving you more centered, at ease, and prepared to tackle the demands that you will face throughout the day.

Step Three: Raising and Lowering Your Anxiety Level at Will.

After familiarizing yourself with the relaxation technique of your choice, you can use it along with your calm scene to create a feeling of serenity which can counteract anxious feelings whenever you feel them stirring.

First, practice. Once you are physically relaxed and your breathing is slow and steady, conjure up your calm scene, drinking in every detail of it. Stay in that place of peace and serenity for as long as you like. You are at ground zero as far as your anxiety is concerned. After you open your eyes, spend a few minutes remembering the feeling of physical relaxation and mental calm you just experienced. Several times a day for the next few days, stop for a moment and recall those sensations again. Notice that you can re-create them at will.

Once you feel fairly confident of your ability to relax and visualize a calm scene, it is time to add a new element. Bring yourself down to ground zero. When you feel very calm and relaxed, begin thinking about something that makes you anxious (an upcoming event, an ongoing problem, an embarrassing moment, a painful memory). Allow your anxiety to reach level number three on a one to ten scale, *then switch your attention back to your breathing, your body, and your calm scene until you have returned to ground zero once again.* Repeat the process over as many days as it takes to get yourself all the way up to level ten and back down to zero.

If you keep practicing this technique, you will make an amazing discovery. It starts getting *easier* to reduce your anxiety and *more difficult* to reach the top of your anxiety rating scale. You have literally gotten better at being relaxed than at being overwhelmed by anxiety—and you can carry your newly developed ability to reduce anxiety with you into your daily affairs. In fact, as soon as you feel yourself getting anxious, you can center yourself by taking a few deep breaths, tensing-holding-relaxing your neck or shoulder muscles and thinking briefly about your calm scene. It will take you no more than a few seconds and no one will even know that you are doing it.

LONG-RANGE ATTITUDE CHANGES

The cognitive maneuvers I just described enable you to cut anxiety off at the pass as soon as you feel it. However, there are also steps you can take to be less prone to anxiety in general. Here are some of the measures that I highly recommend.

Accept more, expect less. If you can learn to recognize and accept your limitations and accept other people as individuals (with their own limitations), you automatically become more flexible and less anxious during difficult interactions and in stressful situations.

What do I mean by acceptance? "Getting" the whole picture. Being able to say, "This is what is happening right now. This is what I think and how I feel about it. This is why. I may not like it, but I am aware of what is involved, what I can influence and what I cannot." When you reach that point, you can decide whether you will try to live with those circumstances ("I know what's going on and it's okay" or "It's not okay but I am not prepared to do anything about them right now") or attempt to change them.

What is there to accept? That certain circumstances and certain personality traits (both your own and other people's) are unlikely to change in the foreseeable future. That certain elements of any situation are truly beyond your control and that you will only drive yourself crazy by trying to control them or make them change. That you are allowed to be where you are at any given moment. You can learn to accept that when you and others view a given situation differently, neither one of you is necessarily a powerless victim or a malicious villain. Indeed, you might even consider the possibility that other people—whom you once perceived as evil, cruel, or idiotic—are actually unaware of their effect on you, are vulnerable because of their own insecurities and unmet needs, or lack the skills and insights to conduct themselves differently.

To cultivate a more accepting attitude, start jettisoning some of your "shoulds," "have tos," "musts," and "I'm entitled tos"; in other words some of your expectations, your assumptions about what is *supposed to* happen and what you believe is owed to you. Instead of approaching interactions and relationships with the preconceived notion that they should proceed in a certain way and *cannot be any other way,* try to determine what you wish or want to happen. Then put your hopes and desires through a reality test, asking yourself:

- Exactly what do I want from this person or situation? (Be as clear and specific as possible.)
- Why do I want it? What are my real motives?
- *In this situation at this time,* can my wishes actually be fulfilled?

While you still may end up being disappointed, by adjusting your agenda to actual circumstances, you are less likely to become outraged or depressed or jump to the conclusion that you or others have screwed up and must pay for that transgression.

Don't put all your eggs in one basket. Instead of relying on just your job, your spouse, your children, your best friend, or any one person or situation to meet all or most of your needs, seek out and take advantage of a number of different sources of satisfaction. Get into therapy, join a support group, become more active in your church or synagogue, volunteer, take adult education courses, get a part-time job, a pen pal, a hobby. The more diversified your interests, the less enmeshed with one person or tangled up in one situation you will be. But more importantly, because your needs are being met elsewhere, you lose your sense of desperation, your tendency to cling to and worry about losing that individual or those circumstances.

Give yourself permission to be "bad." An enormous amount of our anxiety stems from worrying about doing the right thing. More often than not picking up where our parents left off, our consciences perpetually remind us to be "good" and warn us of the dire consequences we will suffer if we "misbehave." Some of these taboos serve a positive purpose and prevent us from hurting ourselves or others. However, many of the rules we live by do not actually apply to our adult lives and some we follow too rigidly, adhering to them even when they are not helping us in any way. It is incredibly liberating to break a few rules from time to time. In fact, doing so is the only way to learn that it is okay to:

- not be helpful to everyone all of the time;
- say "no" when "no" is what you mean;
- make mistakes;
- change your mind;
- go with your gut feelings occasionally instead of striving to be logical and rational at all times.

Try letting yourself off the hook now and then. Give yourself permission to be "bad," not to do the "right" thing. Whether or not you take advantage of the opportunity to break the rules, you will find that knowing you could if you wanted to lifts a tremendous weight off your shoulders.

Take care of yourself. Take the time to relax. Exercise on a regular basis. Spend time with people you like. Reassure yourself. Make a list of your accomplishments, the countless things that you could not do when you were ten years old but which you can do now. Read that list at least once a day and any time you feel insecure or inadequate. Keep track of your successes, no matter how small or insignificant they seem. Start an inventory today, adding to it each time you set a goal and reach it, choose a new approach and use it, handle a baffling situation effectively and so on. Since it is much easier to tolerate anxiety when you are physically healthy and on an even emotional keel, these measures, which relieve stress and enhance self-esteem, are extremely beneficial.

Once you have developed a more positive attitude toward change and increased your tolerance for anxiety, you can actually get off auto-pilot and begin generating new alternatives as well as making new choices.

How to Change

As one of the positive thoughts found in the previous chapter pointed out, no matter how messy, unsatisfying, or downright depressing your present circumstances are, you do not have to change *everything* about yourself. You have countless characteristics, attitudes, and attributes that are fine and working for you just the way they are.

Take out a sheet of paper and about two thirds of the way down the page, draw a horizontal line. Fill in the top section with anything that you do like about yourself or your life today. Include your strong points, talents, skills, personality traits, the people, activities and things that you feel good about, relationships that you value and so on. Unlike the list of your accomplishments that I mentioned just earlier, this list will serve to point out the various aspects of your nature that cannot necessarily be measured in terms of accomplishments.

Fill in the bottom section with situations or interactions that you feel you handle effectively—those that you feel confident about and, more often than not, walk away from feeling satisfied with the outcome. To qualify for your list, the situation or interaction need not be big or earth-shattering. If dealing with a toddler's temper tantrums or getting your doctor to explain exactly what she is doing is something you do well, put it on the list.

Of course, there are also aspects of yourself or your circumstances that you do not particularly care for and habits or tendencies that do not work in your best interest.

On another sheet of paper that is divided in the same way as the last, fill the top section with anything that you do not like about yourself or your circumstances. Include weakness; limitations; sore spots; bad habits; baffling behaviors; people, activities, and things that you do not feel good about; relationships that are not working and so on. To compensate for the natural tendency to see every flaw but be blind to your positive attributes, do not let this list grow longer than the list of things you do like. If it does, go back and add more to the other list.

Fill the bottom section with situations and interactions that tend to baffle you or make you feel anxious and that you believe you do not handle effectively.

Now go back over both lists, marking each item with an A, B, or C—A for anything that is a very important and integral part of your life today (something you cherish and would fight to keep or something that makes you miserable and you would wish it away if you could); B for anything that has an impact but not as great an impact as an A item; and C for anything that is not particularly important to you (keeping or getting rid of it would not make that much difference to you).

After you have done that, get a third sheet of paper and draw a vertical line down the middle of it. From the A items on your "like" page, choose ten things that are of the utmost importance to you, things that you want to keep the way they are or get or be more of. List them in descending order in the left-hand column.

From the A, B, or C items on your "don't like" page, choose five that you would most like to change and five that seem as if they would be the easiest to change. List them in any order in the right-hand column.

You now have a framework for deciding *what* you want to change and *how* you want to change it. You have a list of positive attributes and abilities which you can draw upon while you change. And a list of undesirable habits or tendencies which you can replace with whatever attitudes and behaviors you consciously choose to adopt. From these lists, you can begin to develop goals, the end results you hope to achieve by changing yourself or your circumstances.

Although you will no longer use some of your old methods or use them less often than you did in the past, you get to keep them. You can go back to your old ways whenever you want to—if you want to—and you may, under certain circumstances. Contrary to the widely held notion, when you choose to change, you *do not give up anything.* You *exchange* one set of attitudes and behaviors for another. You achieve this by:

- doing or being *more* of what you like (spending more time with your children, being more creative at work, or taking up hobbies that tap into your creativity);

- doing or being *less* of what you don't like (cutting down the number of nights you spend watching TV, people pleasing less often);
- staying the same in certain situations and relationships but not in others (listening to your spouse's problems but not your boss's and all of your coworkers', being spontaneous and going with the flow on the weekends but planning ahead and sticking to a schedule during the work week);
- transfer skills that help you handle some situations well to the situations you do not handle as well (if you can plan a budget for your department at work, why not do that with your spouse and curtail those money arguments by setting aside in advance certain funds for certain things; if you can let what your in-laws say roll off your back, why not pretend that your annoying officemate is your mother- or father-in-law and use the same approach with him or her?);
- celebrating your strengths and seeking out situations in which you can use them to your own and others' advantage (if you are good with children, get a job working with them or do volunteer work; if you are athletic, start a company softball team or teach aerobics to your coworkers during the lunch hour);
- accepting your limitations and changing your circumstances (if you come unglued whenever you have to do more than two things at once, that job as a receptionist for a public health clinic is not for you; if you are a neatnick and your roommate is a hopeless slob, perhaps it's time to find a new roommate or a new place to live).

With these possibilities in mind and your personal inventory on hand, establish three goals for yourself—with at least one relating to a situation or relationship you have been having difficulty handling effectively. You are not committing yourself to them, but merely identifying ways in which changing yourself or your circumstances could make a difference. Here are several examples contributed by people you have already read about:

KATE:	I want to give people and especially Michael the silent treatment less often and if possible not at all.
STEPH- ANIE:	I want to change careers and get into a helping profession. That way I'll get paid for what I'm good at and can maybe stop taking care of everyone and everything all of the time.
BARRY:	I want to stop trying to figure out what makes Eddie tick and start figuring out how to improve services in my department.
JENNY:	I want to give my software presentations without getting off track.

How will Kate, Stephanie, Barry, and Jenny get from where they are now to where they want to be? How will you? With your vision of your future self or circumstances to guide you, you will generate options, evaluate them, and consciously choose the path you want to take to reach your goal. You will do this not just once, but many times over. This conscious decision-making process—once you learn it— will serve you whenever you encounter one of the countless baffling situations of everyday life.

How to Generate Alternatives

Use your imagination. Learn to brainstorm, to generate a long list of alternatives including everything from the sublime to the ridiculous. Be playful, even silly. After all, you do not have to use the options, only accumulate them. In fact, at this stage, don't evaluate or eliminate anything. Alternatives that *can* work but are often overlooked include doing nothing for now, asking for time to think, or accepting and learning to live with the unchangeable or uncontrollable elements of a situation. And remember that your characteristic response remains an option, since it does work in certain situations (and is not an auto-pilot behavior when you consciously choose to use it).

Locate your transferable skills. Finding new ways to use the skills and positive attributes you already have enables you to further increase your options. A sense of humor, for instance, is particularly useful in baffling or disheartening situations. If you have a great one, a good one, or even a so-so one, instead of going on an eating binge or isolating yourself from all members of the opposite sex after a horrendous experience on a blind date or at a sales presentation, you can look for the humorous aspects of that experience. You can laugh about the absurdity of it or even create a comic monologue to use when relating your experience to your friends.

Are you well organized and a good planner at work? Could you transfer those skills to social situations or your home life, planning dates or parties that include activities you enjoy and feel comfortable doing—in order to compensate for your fear of running out of things to say? Or what about setting up a schedule that gets all family members involved in running the household so that you feel less overwhelmed, exhausted, and resentful?

Return to your inventory and review your "like" list.

Come up with ways to overcome your limitations by building on your strengths.

Conduct surveillances. Begin paying more attention to other people's behavior, especially people whom you admire, respect, or wish to emulate in any way. If you are timid, watch people who are gregarious. If you are passive or reluctant to assert yourself, keep an eye on take-charge people who routinely do the things that you find so difficult. Add your observations to your brainstorm list.

Ask for advice. It's tough to be objective when your own life or relationships seem to be on the line. Other people can offer you a fresh perspective. When you are smack dab in the middle of a baffling situation or bewildering problem, it is extremely difficult to imagine ever getting through it. Yet other people have had and gotten beyond the same trouble spots that have you stymied. You can take advantage of what they learned through experience. People who have skills or knowledge that you lack or who simply operate from a different frame of reference can share options that would never occur to you. You do not have to use the advice you receive, but asking for it expands your horizons and is well worth the pride you may have to swallow.

Once you have explored the numerous options available to you, it is time to conscientiously evaluate them. After eliminating the illegal, immoral, and truly impossible, try one of the following methods for determining which course of action is most likely to fulfill your agenda without hurting you, others, or your ongoing relationships.

How to Evaluate Your Options

Debits and Credits. For each potentially viable option, create a tally sheet. Draw a line down the middle of a sheet of paper to make two columns, one for debits and the other for credits. In the debit column, list the negative consequences you might suffer by pursuing that option. In the credit column, list the positive outcomes you might obtain. Think carefully about your circumstances and then mark with an asterisk (*) the realistic items in each column (those that could actually come to pass rather than those that a bit of psychological spot checking will show are by-products of your old agenda, negative self-concept, or a rigid worldview).

If comparing tally sheets at this point does not cause one option to jump out at you, go back and give a numerical value to each *realistic* consequence or outcome. Use a one to five scale, with five representing the most important consideration and one representing the least important factor. Any option with a lot of highly ranked negative consequences (things that could go wrong or hurt you which would be a big deal for you) probably is not in your best interest. Mediocre rankings in both columns indicate a fairly safe option, but not necessarily one for which you can generate much enthusiasm. The clear winner is usually the option with a number of highly ranked positive outcomes (things you could get and in fact strongly desire) and few important negative consequences.

Because of the complexity of this method and the amount of time it requires, it is most useful for making future plans or major decisions.

The Wish List. Think carefully about what you want to get from a particular situation or relationship. Identify the *ultimate* outcome—the one that would be absolutely perfect in every imaginable way—and the bottom line—the least you would accept and still have your needs met. Some options will help you reach your *bottom* line at the very most. Some may lead to the ultimate outcome. But most will net you results that fall somewhere in between, fulfilling some but not all of your agenda items.

Either visualize or draw a continuum (as on pp. 49–50), a line with the ultimate outcome at one end and your bottom line at the other. Determine where each of your options falls on the continuum. Unless they would create additional problems or cause harm, the alternatives that land closest to the ultimate end of the line are the ones that are likely to be in your best interest.

The Feel-Right Method. Sometimes an option simply feels right. The moment you hear it, your gut instincts tell you that it could work and that you would feel comfortable pursuing it. Or the idea seems to stand out on the page, and throughout your logical analysis you keep coming back to it. Chances are that it is worth a try *if* it is a response other than your characteristic one (habits feel right because you are so used to them) and *if* it does not have a high potential for hurting anyone including yourself (some pretty rotten alternatives feel right in the heat of battle or after someone has "done you wrong").

How Finally to Decide

Having identified the options that are doable and in your best interest, it is time to actually make a choice and act on it. When that time comes, you will undoubtedly notice your resistance to change reemerging and your anxiety level rising. Use what you learned in the last chapter to stop spinning your wheels and start moving down the path you have chosen. Return to and review your personal inventory, bolstering your confidence by reminding yourself of your strong points.

Experiment. Pick a low-risk situation and do something atypical. Change seats on the train when someone wearing too much cologne sits down next to you. Tell a friend who wants to meet you at noon that you'd prefer to meet at 12:30. Put a ranting and raving customer on hold while you regain your composure. Instead of yelling back, tell your ranting and raving teenaged daughter that you might be able to help her or even be willing to give her what she wants if she would calm down and explain herself clearly. Play with your noncharacteristic responses. You might be surprised to discover what happens: that other people react differently than you expected and nothing as disastrous as you imagined actually occurs as a result of this new behavior.

Act *as if* you are already comfortable with your new approach. Consciously pretend that you are already the person you want to be. If you want to move up the career ladder, act as if you already have, dressing the part, offering suggestions, taking the initiative to do more than the bare minimum. If you want to be more self-confident, pretend that you already are. Change your body language. Force yourself to make eye contact instead of sheepishly staring at your fingernails or the floor. Express opinions and make decisions, beginning with small ones like commenting on a movie you have recently seen or picking the restaurant you and your spouse will eat at on Saturday night. As you get more and more comfortable about behaving confidently, you will start to notice that you also feel more confident.

Take one step at a time. Jenny, for instance, did not go directly from losing control of her presentations to remaining composed and in control throughout them. Indeed, many of her early steps did not have a measurable impact on her job performance at all. She had to concentrate on gaining insight and managing her symptoms of stress before she could actually change the habit that was making her miserable. And even that change came in stages. First she got through one section of her outline before responding to questions from her audience. Then she took and answered questions at the end of each hour. Finally, she built into her presentation fifteen-minute free-discussion sessions and small-group activities that enabled her to move around the room and address individual concerns. Although Jenny identified all of these options early on, she implemented them one at a time, and if a step made her unduly anxious or seemed not to be working, she moved back to the previous step until she felt ready to move on again.

That leads to an extremely important point. No decision that you make is etched in stone. There is no path you can choose to travel now that you cannot also choose to turn off of later in your journey. Although you can expect to hear some anxious internal voice asking, *"What if I make the wrong choice?,"* the fact of the matter is that there are no wrong choices or at least none that are so wrong that you cannot learn something from them and *make another choice.* Unlike your automatic behaviors or characteristic responses, your conscious decisions are not prone to getting locked in. Because you know what you are doing and why, if your agenda still is not being fulfilled, you are less likely to keep doing the same thing over and over again. Instead, you will stop, take stock, figure out what's really going on, reconsider your options, and make another decision.

Once you get this far, once you know how to and actually begin to break your self-defeating patterns, including your hiding habit, you are ready to conquer the final frontier —coping with and counteracting other people's hidden agendas, both in specific situations and ongoing relationships.

9

The Final Frontier

Techniques for Coping with Other People's Agendas

As I mentioned at the very beginning of this book, when you encounter difficult people or situations, there are three approaches you can take. You can *change yourself,* you can *change your circumstances,* or you can *drive yourself crazy* by operating on auto-pilot (then beating yourself up about it) or by trying to change the elements of your situation that are truly beyond your control—most notably other people. This chapter provides practical suggestions for doing more of the first two so that you can do less of the third.

You now have all the clues you need to crack the code in which baffling situations are written, to figure out what is really going on below the surface. In addition to gathering pertinent information, coping also involves sharing your concerns and receiving comfort; redefining situations in order to make them more manageable; considering alternatives and examining consequences. You know how to do that too. You are already armed with the insight and tools you need to handle baffling situations, and could go out and act in your own best interest right this very minute.

When I suggest this to my patients, they rarely believe me. They still have a few questions for me to answer, a few pointers they'd like me to give them—and you may too. Following are the questions I am most often asked when therapy sessions, lectures, or casual conversations turn to the topic of hidden agendas, and these are the suggestions I most often offer in response.

How Can I Keep People from Manipulating Me?

Although you cannot prevent people from *trying* to con you into doing what they want you to do, you *can* make it more difficult for their manipulations to succeed. Start by becoming more familiar with your *exploitable points*—the buttons manipulators push to stir up the anxiety, self-doubt, and anger that prompts you to automatically respond in precisely the way they want you to. Here are some commonly exploited vulnerabilities and the darts manipulators aim at them.

Being a People Pleaser. Because you believe that meeting other people's needs and making them happy is the primary or even the only way to maintain a relationship or feel good about yourself, you are one big button just waiting to be pushed and will almost always do almost anything others want you to do. Watch out for lines like, "I know you won't let me down," "I can always count on you," "True friends (loyal employees, good sports) like you are so hard to find," and "I don't know what I'd do without you," as well as sulking, sighing, and hard-luck stories.

Guilt. The slightest hint that you have done or are doing something wrong compels you to make amends by giving in to the person who is pushing your guilt button. You fall for lines like "It's okay. (sigh) I understand that you . . . ," "I'm sure you didn't mean it, but . . . ," "Haven't I always . . ." followed by reminders of how well they have always treated you, "When you needed . . . , didn't I . . ." (pointing out past favors or sacrifices, often followed by "and did I complain?") and many more.

Fear of Conflict. You go out of your way to avoid arguments or dissension of any kind. The manipulator will get to you by acting irritated or on the verge of exploding (pounding a desk, slamming doors, rolling his eyes in exasperation, glaring at you) and making comments like, "I'm sure you'll agree that . . . ," "*We* have a problem," "Let me make my position perfectly clear," "If you don't like it, speak up now," and "I don't want to start an argument, but . . ."

Wanting to Fit In. Thriving on the acceptance of your peers and the approval of authority figures or others you admire, you are putty in the hands of a manipulator who thwarts your need to create the right impression or blend into the crowd. Watch out for bosses or colleagues, who during a meeting single you out and ask, "What do you think about this?" (They may be trying to get someone to agree with or compliment them and will probably succeed.) Other manipulators might do something they know embarrasses you or make references to previous embarrassing incidents. You are also susceptible to comments like, "Everyone I've spoken to agrees that . . . ," "I know what a team player you are," and "As I'm sure you know . . ."

Silence. If someone does not respond to you immediately, you are likely to feel rejected or automatically assume that they disapprove of what you did or said, are thinking of a tactful way to criticize you, or are upset and expect you to make them feel all better. Watch out for sulkers and pouters (you'll buy right into their game of hide-and-go-seek) and authority figures who stare you down, never crack a smile, or continue whatever they are doing even though you are obviously waiting for them to acknowledge your presence or respond to your comments.

Perfectionism. You are driven to succeed at all you do, hate making mistakes, and tend to take on more burdens than any mere mortal could possibly handle. Since you are sensitive to criticism or the slightest intimation that you might not be "up to" a task, be on the lookout for comments like "I know how busy you are, but . . . ," "Maybe I'm asking too much of you, but . . . ," "All things considered, you did a great job, however . . . ," or "It isn't how I would have handled it, but . . ." When people who typically make demands express concern ("You look tired," "Are you spreading yourself too thin?" "Maybe you should slow down"), they may actually be hoping you'll say, "Really, I'm fine," so they can make a demand, or may be trying to get you to give up some other responsibility so that you can take on the one they want you to assume.

Competitiveness. You love to win or hate to lose and are apt to judge yourself by ticking off the ways you are better than others. You are an easy mark for comparisons ("The person who had this job before you . . . ," "Your brother finds time to . . . ," "The Joneses have . . . ," "You're the only parents in America who don't . . .") and attempts to make you jealous (flirting with others, flaunting a new possession, whispering to a coworker while glancing in your direction or sharing inside information that you feel you should have been privy to).

A Short Fuse. If you are easily angered, a master manipulator first sets you off by needling or teasing you, being late, embarrassing you, or giving you inside information about something someone else did or said. Then, playing the role of the injured party ("What did I do to deserve that?" "You're too sensitive. I was only joking"), they get you to make amends. Or they become an instant ally, sympathizing with you and suggesting a way to handle the situation—which is apt to be something they wanted you to do in the first place. Watch out for passive aggressors. They'll get you every time.

Being Easily Flattered. Most of us are, of course. However, some of us—especially those of us who feel insecure or suffer from low self-esteem—are so thrilled and grateful to be praised or recognized in any positive way that we want to immediately repay the favor. We have been softened up and are primed for the kill. Or we may so hunger for recognition, fame, or status that we feel invulnerable, as in: "They said they'd never heard such an inspiring sales talk!" "He couldn't have done it without me." "Boy, I was terrific!" When the inevitable flaw appears, our balloon is punctured, we fall from on high. And it *is* inevitable—for we all have flaws.

Make Yourself Less Exploitable

Once you become aware of your exploitable points, you can use a bit of preventive medicine in order to provide manipulators with less ammunition to use against you. Until you are aware of how people operate or have some sense that you can trust them, be selective about the personal information you reveal to them. Be a little *less* open when it comes to your vulnerabilities. And learn from your experiences.

It's counterproductive to beat yourself up with such thoughts as "I blew it." That just compounds the problem; instead, be kind to yourself. Then if you realize in retrospect that you have been manipulated, think about the interaction, identify the bait that the manipulator used to hook you, and figure out how he or she reeled you in. In time, as you encounter those tactics you will know what is happening *while it is happening*—and while you can still do something about it.

What can you do? First, you can acknowledge to yourself that you are being manipulated and how you feel about it. ("She's pushing my guilt button and it's getting to me. I feel guilty and I'm telling myself that I must be a lousy friend for not wanting to go to lunch with her.") Then you can use the talk-back technique or other cognitive maneuvers to restore your equilibrium. ("I'm not a lousy friend. I just happen to be too busy to go to lunch today.")

In the midst of a hidden-agenda interaction, this may be difficult to do. However, there is no law saying that you must always respond immediately. Ask for time to think things over or find a way to physically remove yourself from the situation for a few minutes. If you feel cornered and can think of no other way to buy yourself some thinking time, excuse yourself to use the rest room. As I like to tell my patients, everyone is allowed to do that and unless you are excusing yourself every ten minutes, no one will question it.

Figure out what manipulators are trying to get you to do. Do they want you to agree with them, tell them something they want to hear, accept an assignment that you do not actually want, or *not* say what you planned to say? How much will you regret or resent doing what they want? What might the consequences be if you do not? Would it make you feel better or prevent future manipulations if you let them know that you are onto them? Once you address those questions, you can:

1. Say nothing about their methods and consciously choose (rather than automatically agree) to do what they are trying to get you to do.
2. Say nothing about their methods and stick to your guns.
3. Confront them directly. ("I'm feeling manipulated. Is there something you aren't telling me?")
4. Confront or deflect their maneuver with humor. ("You wouldn't be trying to guilt me into this, would you?" "Hmmm. If I'm that indispensable, maybe I should ask for a raise." "You actually surveyed every parent in America? I'm impressed.")
5. Agree to do what they want you to do, but let them know that you know what they are up to. ("Sure, I'll help you out this time, but don't take that to mean I fell for that hard-luck story." "I'd be glad to do that—and you know what, I would also have done it if you just came right out and asked me to.")
6. Agree with the point they made in hopes of manipulating you and then say no or offer an alternative. ("You're right. I am a team player and that's why I'll sit this one out and give another player a chance to bat." "It's true that my brother would find time to do it, but right now I can't." "You know, I *have* been spreading myself too thin, so I think I'd better not take on this particular project.")

Learn to Decode and
Neutralize Mixed Messages

Manipulators frequently use mixed messages to get their point across without having to own up to it, to get a rise out of you, to punish you for unspecified transgressions, or to obtain comfort and reassurance without acknowledging their need for it. They get their own way because you automatically respond to what is *not* being said rather than what is. If you take out your code book and decipher the covert message you are receiving, you can avoid getting hooked by it. Here are a few familiar mixed messages and what they usually mean.

Words: "Anything you want."
Translation: "I'm not willing to make a decision, but I'll end up complaining about the one you make."

Words: "We'll see."
Translation: "Forget it," or "I've already made up my mind, but I won't reveal my decision until it's too late to discuss it," or "I know you want this and I'll probably give it to you, but first I want to see you sweat."

Words: "Could you do me a favor?"
Translation: "I am about to make an unreasonable request and get away with it because your automatic reply to my question was 'sure.' "

Words: "Far be it from me to say . . . ," "I'm no expert, but . . . ," or "I don't want to tell you what to do, but . . ."
Translation: "I'm about to tell you what to do, and you'd better do it."

Words: "I think we all agree . . ."
Translation: "You're going to look like an idiot (or I'm

going to get angry at you) if you disagree with what I am about to say."

Words: "I looked fat." "I blew it, didn't I?" "Did I make a fool of myself?"
Translation: "Please tell me that I didn't."

Words: "Don't get me wrong . . ."
Translation: "I'm about to say something that you won't like, but if you don't like it, I'm going to deny that I meant it."

Words: "Well, I don't know . . ." (trailing off and usually accompanied by an upward gaze or head shaking).
Translation: "I think you're making a big mistake."

Words: "If that's what you want (sigh)."
Translation: "I don't want that, but I'll give in and go along with it. I will also find a way to make you pay for it."

Words: "I guess you know what you're doing."
Translation: "Why don't you come to your senses and do it my way."

Of course there are many other examples, most notably *loaded questions* like "Wouldn't it be better if . . . ?" "Why don't you . . . ?" "Shouldn't we try to . . . ?" and "Aren't you being . . . ?" These aren't questions at all, but rather thinly disguised opinions or demands. In addition, when there are discrepancies between *what* is being said and *how* it is being said, the nonverbal message usually reflects the speaker's true meaning.

Once you have decoded a mixed message, you can choose to:

1. Respond to the real message—
　　Their words: "Well, I don't know . . ."
　　Your response: "I've given this a lot of thought

and want to do it this way. If I make a mistake, I'll deal with it."

> *Their words:* "If that's what you want."
> *Your response:* "You don't have to go along with what I want. Let's discuss it."

2. Consciously pretend that the covert message does not exist and respond to the overt one—

> *Their words:* "I think we all agree."
> *Your response:* "Excuse me. I believe there are still a few points to discuss."

> *Their words:* "Anything you want."
> *Your response:* "Okay, I want. . . . If you have any objections, tell me now."

3. Let it roll off your back and say nothing.

4. Acknowledge the setup and offer an alternative. For example, Michael decided to respond to the mixed messages he received from Kate by saying, "When I asked you if you were upset, you said that you weren't, but your actions seem to be signaling that you are. I am going to believe what you told me and won't ask again. However, if you decide to tell me that something is bothering you and what it is, I *will* try to give you whatever you need."

5. Return the ball to their court by asking a direct question that may bring the covert message out into the open. For instance, when Jane set up her daughter, Sara, by asking, "Don't you have the oven temperature set too high?" Sara could have asked, "Do you think I have it set too high?" Or if someone uses the "If that's what you want" mixed message, you might respond by asking, "What do *you* want?" (Of course, an astute power player is apt to say, "I don't know," in which case, you'll have to try one of the other approaches.)

6. Accept that this is how the other people operate and give them the reassurance they need (or any other response that does not require too large a sacrifice on your part).

As you no doubt noticed, several of the options I suggested in this section involved doing what the manipulator intended for you to do all along. Wouldn't that mean you *had* been manipulated? you may wonder. Wouldn't you be letting the manipulator get away with his or her hidden-agenda power play? No, you wouldn't. You would have consciously chosen to do whatever was in your best interest at that time and in that situation. And that is a far cry from automatically doing what they wanted you to do simply because they had pushed your buttons.

How Can I Get Rid of the Hidden Agendas in My Relationships?

You can't. Not all of them anyway, and as I have stressed at various points throughout this book, even if you could, it would not necessarily be in your best interest to do so. On the other hand, you *can* break out of rigid relationship patterns, bring hidden sources of conflict out into the open and learn to communicate in ways that are less likely to trigger characteristic responses or activate unconscious coping mechanisms.

These options—which I will get to shortly—involve changing *your* actions and reactions. By doing so, you alter the way in which you and people involved in relationships with you interact. However, it is only fair to warn you that this is neither an easy nor a foolproof approach. While changing your attitudes and behaviors always affects the people in your life, it does not mean that *they* will change at all or in the way you wish they would. Nothing you can do can make other people change. Nor can you make them like or even begrudgingly accept the new you. You can, however, be prepared for their resistance and cope with it.

When You Change but They Won't (or Don't Want You To)

- "You aren't the person I married."
- "What's happened to you?"
- "That never used to bother you."
- "This isn't like you."
- "You're ruining everything."

These are the sounds of discontent made by spouses, friends, parents, children, colleagues, or others who are reacting to changes in your attitude or behavior. They are the words you will hear whenever people who have relationships with you dig in their heels and use every trick in the book to get you to return to your old, familiar, predictable way of operating in that relationship. Most of the people in your life will react in this manner at least initially and sometimes indefinitely.

The loudest protests and most determined attempts to preserve the status quo will come from people who feel as if the new you and the new rules for relating to you are being forced upon them and that you violated their psychological contract by failing to consult them about decisions that affect them. If that is in fact the case, then their knee-jerk reaction is understandable. However, they may feel this way even though you *did* consult them before going into therapy, implementing the taskforce's recommendations, or otherwise changing yourself or your circumstances. They may act as if you have committed an unpardonable sin even though they originally agreed with and supported your decision. More baffling still, they may try to sabotage you even though you are doing exactly what they have been encouraging and even nagging you to do for years.

For instance, a young woman's parents, who once dedicated themselves to getting her married off and used to think any single man who could still breathe on his own was a suitable mate, begin complaining about her lovers as soon as they realize that a relationship is getting serious. "You could do better," they say or repeatedly warn her not to "rush into anything." Their bewildering turnaround is prompted by their delayed and largely unconscious realization that should their daughter actually marry, she might not need or have time for them anymore.

Like these parents, anyone in your life who initially supports your decision to change or even suggests that you change may not anticipate the extent to which *your* new attitudes and behavior will affect *them*. They know what you intend to do, but they may not understand what it means. Only after you change does it dawn on them that they stand to lose something to which they were accustomed—a way of perceiving and relating to you that was familiar to them and therefore comfortable and safe. They can no longer accurately predict what you will do in any given situation or be sure that you will be there for them at all.

Even more disturbing, when you change your characteristic responses to people with whom you have relationships, your new attitudes and behavior make their typical attitudes and behavior obsolete. Their strategic maneuvers become less effective. Their preconceived notions about who you are and what you are supposed to do no longer fit. They must adapt accordingly. They must change, and if you can remember how reluctant you were to do that, you can also understand how they might be just as reluctant—and more so if they did not see your changes coming. As a result and in spite of all evidence to the contrary, they will wholeheartedly believe that your life together *used to be* idyllic and try to make "right" again the relationship that they think you turned upside down. At best they will respond unenthusiastically to the new you or refuse to take you seriously and they may even demand that you change back. Before you decide that they are out to get you, maliciously trying to thwart you or expecting you to sacrifice your happiness for theirs, give them some time to adjust and overcome their own instinctive resistance to change. You can also:

- Be clear about your own motives. Are you changing because you believe that doing so will force the other person in the relationship to change? Do you think they will have no choice but to treat you differently once you show them that you are different? Are you hoping to please them, to become the person you think they want you to be in order to get the affection, respect, recognition, or attention you have not gotten from them in the past? If so, you are setting yourself up for disappointment. What's more, you will easily be convinced to return to your old ways even though they were not working (and still won't).

- Whenever feasible, let significant others know what you have in mind—both what you plan to do and why you want to do it. It will not serve you to be punitive about this. Informing others that you are "mad as hell and cannot take it anymore," that they made you do something or drove you to it increases resistance rather than decreases it.

- Acknowledge that adjusting to these changes may not be easy for either of you.

- Ask for their help and/or support. This may involve

anything from bearing with you while you implement a new computer system that will initially require *more* time but will eventually reduce the time required to process everyone's paperwork, to assuming more responsibility for the household while you spend more time elsewhere. Enlist others in generating options and give them room to make their own choices about *how* they can be supportive.

- When you do encounter resistance, avoid accusing others of trying to sabotage you (even if that is what they are doing). Use the communication tools that you will find later in this chapter to go back to square one and restate your position calmly, explain how and why their behavior is not helpful and offer alternatives.
- Recognize that ending that relationship or temporarily discontinuing it may become an option, especially when you feel good about the changes in yourself but the other person more and more adamantly opposes them.

With these realities in mind, let's move on to the two most destructive side effects of hidden agendas in ongoing relationships—rigid relationship patterns and recurring conflicts—and what you can do about them.

Breaking Out of a Rigid Relationship Pattern

Whether you are caught up in Hide and Go Seek, Mother May I, Getting Even, Making It All Better or any other gamelike relationship pattern I described earlier, to break out of the self-defeating cycle of moves and countermoves you must *stop playing by the old rules.* Whether the other player is your spouse, boss, parent, child, coworker, neighbor, or friend, when it is your turn to make a move, *make a different move than your typical one.* Here are several examples.

Instead of jumping the gun and immediately trying to make others "all better," invite them to talk about what is bothering them or do nothing until they volunteer that information.

Instead of collecting injustices and marching them all out during one monster argument, or getting even, calmly express your feelings about the behavior when or soon after it occurs, and in a nondemanding way specify what you wish that person had done or would do in the future.

Instead of dismissing the injustice collector's complaints as the ravings of a lunatic, try saying something like "I'm hearing about a lot of things I've done over a long period of time. Until now, I didn't realize that they bothered you. Since I'm pretty sure I can't fix all of them and don't know which ones are most important to you, could we discuss just one or two things right now?"

Instead of retaliating after the other person has done something to get even, do *not* retaliate. You may acknowledge that you *feel like* you are being punished and would like to discuss what you might have done so that you can try not to do it again.

Although these few examples contain the alternatives that I have observed to be most helpful, *any* move other than your typical one breaks the pattern, preventing the other person's usual move from having the desired effect. Unfortunately, the previously bottled up and buried fear, anger, or resentment that was the driving force behind your deceptive moves and countermoves is also likely to rise to the surface, causing major conflicts or many minor skirmishes over seemingly unrelated issues. Since suppressed feelings have probably been leaking out in disguised form for quite some time, this will not necessarily be a new development in your relationship—although it may occur more often or with more intensity.

As unpleasant as this prospect may seem, it paves the way for conflicts—especially recurring ones—to be resolved productively. This feat is accomplished by figuring out what you are really fighting about and employing effective communication tools, ones which lead to compromises and psychological contract renegotiations rather than no-win competitions and endlessly trying to get your own way.

Uncovering Hidden Sources of Conflict

Are there recurring conflicts in any of your relationships, trouble spots you wander into over and over again? Do certain discussions invariably lead to full-scale battles, and during those battles, does the intensity of your own or the other person's feelings seem out of proportion to the issue at hand? Do you sometimes look back on an argument and wonder how either or both of you got so worked up over something that seems so trivial or ridiculous in retrospect? Does tension remain in the air for hours or days after a conflict appears to have been resolved? If so, then (yes, you guessed it) a hidden or automatic agenda is operating, and what is being hidden— among other things—is the real issue that is upsetting or threatening one or both of you.

For instance, many recurring conflicts, especially those that are emotionally charged even though there is only a minor difference of opinion, are really about *controlling your destiny,* being able to choose, preventing others from ignoring or questioning your authority, or warding off frightening feelings of powerlessness. This was certainly the case for one of my patients who became incensed every time her boyfriend wasted food. She was convinced that she would not be able to fully commit herself to him or their relationship until he got rid of that infuriating habit of his. "His eyes are bigger than his stomach," she explained. "He goes to a salad bar and piles things on his plate, things he doesn't even know if he likes. Of course, he ends up throwing half of it away. When we barbecue, I have to slice the steak and give it to him one piece at a time. Otherwise he'd take twice as much as he could possibly eat." She can easily come up with at least two dozen more examples of his seemingly stubborn refusal to live up to what she considers a cardinal rule: "You can take what you want, but you have to eat what you take."

Worse yet, he does not take his concern about this matter seriously. "He laughs at me," she says indignantly. "He thinks it's some silly quirk I have. But I'm serious. How can I marry him if he keeps doing it? What if he passes it on to our children?"

Although this patient insists (and her boyfriend confirms) that the only thing that they repeatedly argue about is wasting food, is that really what is preventing her from marrying him? Of course not. She cannot commit herself to her relationship with this lusty man who wants to taste more of life than he can possibly digest. She fears that she will be swept away by his excesses (which at other times she finds sexy, exciting, and fun). She fears losing all control over her environment, something she now needs in order to feel comfortable and secure.

A second hidden source of conflict are *affronts to our self-esteem,* in particular, conditions that prevent us from feeling competent or convince us that we are unappreciated. That was how Eddie felt when he was not promoted into the position that Barry was hired to fill. In his mind, he heard the administration of the hospital where he had worked for seven years saying, "You are nothing. Everything you have done counts for nothing. We don't give a damn about you." And he decided not to give a damn either. He also got angry, starting arguments with Barry at every turn, creating conflicts that could not be resolved because they were not really about what they appeared to be about on the surface.

In order to feel worthwhile, we all need to have some effect on people, get others to hear us out, be given the chance to do things for ourselves and periodically to get our own way. And getting others to make us feel competent, loved, recognized, and valued may be the goals we are really trying to achieve when we repeatedly get into arguments over money, sex, who does the dishes, or what television program to watch, or bicker, gripe, and even go on strike ostensibly over wages or production quotas or the condition of the company lunchroom.

Disillusionment is another hidden source of conflict. If you take a close look at what you now consider to be your lover, spouse, boss, friend, or company's most irritating or infuriating characteristics, you are apt to find that they are the flip side of the attributes that originally attracted you. You are suffering from the "I got what I wanted but it wasn't what I expected" syndrome. You wanted the kind mate you chose, but you didn't expect him to say "All that matters is how you feel about it," each time you sought his opinion. Nor did you expect his kindness to extend to letting your neighbor "get away with" turning his yard into an eyesore—because he does not want to hurt the neighbor's feelings by commenting on it. The behavior you once called kind, you now call wimpy.

Likewise the employee who seemed refreshingly decisive when you hired her is labeled an obstinate shrew once you've worked with her for a while (and realize that you cannot manipulate her into agreeing with your point of view). And the company you chose to join because of its open, familylike atmosphere may now seem smothering and more interested in "making nice" than in competing in the marketplace. Forgetting that *you* bought the whole package, you cannot get over how much *they* have changed—which is why conflicts that are really about disillusionment usually include references to the way the other person "used to" be or accusations concerning what that person "led you to believe."

Some conflicts are the end result of our struggle to define and maintain the amount of *closeness* we can comfortably tolerate in any relationship. We establish a closeness comfort zone that is satisfying and workable for us and whenever we find ourselves outside its boundaries—either closer or more distant than we want or expect to be—we instinctively try to get back to where we need to be. When a wife angrily says to her husband, "You never talk to me," she is really saying, "You are not letting me be as close to you as I want to be." If your teenager is sarcastic, sullenly silent, or accuses you of invading his privacy when all you did was bring his clean laundry into his bedroom, he is telling you that he needs more distance.

Not only do we have conflicts with others over this issue, but we may stir up conflict in order to get others to back off and give us room to breathe. The tension that remains in the air after some "silly little spat" usually keeps others from bothering us for a while and a heated discussion about taking out the garbage or whose turn it is to use the Xerox machine reduces the chance that the other person will ask any probing questions about the dented fender on the family car, your relationship with the executive vice-president of the company or anything else you might want to keep to yourself. Rarely are you consciously aware of doing this, but a close inspection of your behavior patterns may reveal that it is indeed the case.

Depending on others to meet our needs and sensing that they might not can also be the driving force behind recurring conflicts. As one of my colleagues once told me, "My lover could never understand why I got so angry when she left the orange juice out of the refrigerator overnight. I couldn't explain it either until I realized it only bothered me when she had been busy with work for several weeks in a row. I wasn't worried about the orange juice. I was worried that she was going to leave *me* out of her life." You, too, may discover that when *you* feel left out, unsupported, threatened, or insecure, *they* do something that drives you up a wall; something you feel compelled to mention and which starts a fight.

Finally, *psychological contract violations* may be a hidden source of conflict. When the unwritten rules of your relationship are broken, when unspoken expectations are not met, when one person does something that the other believes he or she agreed not to do, all hell can break loose—with at least one and sometimes both of you feeling at a loss to explain what you two are actually fighting about.

I have already provided two strategies for ferreting out the hidden sources of conflict in your relationships. The "What's on your agenda?" questions found in Chapter 4 enable you to identify what you may be transferring from past experiences or previous relationships; what you are telling yourself about yourself that may be distorting your perceptions of the events going on around you and how your worldview and the expectations it contains may be fueling your indignation. The psychological contract worksheet found in Chapter 6 helps pinpoint the rules and norms the other person may have knowingly or unwittingly violated and what you expected to receive from that person but are not getting (and are therefore attempting to wring out of him or her).

Working from that foundation, you can:

- use the talk-back technique and other cognitive maneuvers to regain some control over your runaway emotions as well as gain a more objective perspective on the nature and relative importance of the issue you are fighting about;

- provide the other person with information about some of what is going on inside you (how you are feeling, what memories are stirred up by the present situation, what you are afraid of), thus "owning" your contribution to the conflict and helping the other person better understand your point of view;
- bring more of your psychological contract out into the open, perhaps discussing some of what you uncovered when you completed the worksheet or, when feasible, asking the other person to complete a worksheet, too, and then comparing notes;
- renegotiate your psychological contract, asking and reaching mutually agreeable answers to the following questions:

—What do we expect from each other and this relationship?

—Are those expectations valid now?

—If they were valid in the past but are not now, what changed and how can we alter our expectations accordingly?

—What are we up against?

—What is happening repeatedly?

—What can we do?

—What help do we need?

Of course, these steps are nearly impossible to take in the midst of a heated battle when both of you are flinging accusations, insults, and barbed comments back and forth at one another. Even after the fact, when both of you are calmer and willing to discuss the matter rationally, you can resolve conflicts productively if and only if you communicate effectively.

How to Communicate for Win-Win Conflict Resolution

There are many excellent books available to teach you the ins and outs of effective communication. Rather than trying to give you a crash course, I have listed some of them in Recommended Reading at the end of this book. Here now are what I consider to be the most important ground rules and realities.

1. Think before you speak. You have the *right* to express your feelings and opinions, but also the *responsibility* to present them in a way that is least likely to hurt the other person or push his or her buttons.

2. Say what you mean. Although you need not say every single thing you think or feel, discussions aimed at resolving conflicts are unlikely to achieve that aim if you employ a hidden agenda or use strategic maneuvers to protect yourself or manipulate the other person. This is neither the time nor place for giving hints and then expecting the other person to figure out what is really going on inside you.

3. Use "I" messages and avoid accusations and generalizations. Try not to say things like "You always . . . ," "You never . . . ," "You know what your problem is," "You just don't get it, do you?" or "Why can't you be . . ." They add an unnecessary emotional charge to the interaction (and are not helpful comments under any circumstances). In addition, discuss *specific* needs and behaviors rather than questioning the other person's character or motives.

4. Listen. When the other person is talking, pay attention to what is being said instead of getting ahead of yourself and thinking about what you are going to say in response.

5. Listen *actively*. After the other person finishes speaking, reflect back the message you heard, summarizing or paraphrasing what you think was said. Ask if that is what the other person meant. Once you have restated the message to the other person's satisfaction, respond by expressing your feelings about what you heard as well as your own ideas about the matter.

6. Do not *assume* that the other person understands your point of view or that you understand his or her thoughts and feelings. Even if you've gone over the same ground countless times before, check things out anyway. After all, if either or both of you "got it" before, you would not be discussing it again.

7. Never put words into the other person's mouth. Saying "You think I'm an idiot," or "You're not really angry about that silly thing. You just want me to feel guilty," gets you absolutely nowhere.

8. Specify exactly what the problem or subject under discussion is and stick to it, focusing your attention on that topic rather than bringing up other problems or unresolved feelings from previous conflicts.

9. Skip the question of who is at fault. Blaming and criticizing each other and justifying or defending your own behavior *will not* help you resolve your differences. Acknowledging your feelings about a specific behavior and suggesting alternatives will. Try the following formula:

—I feel . . . (your reaction);
—When you . . . (the specific behavior);
—I would prefer . . . (the alternative);
    and I am willing to . . . (what you would do or stop doing in order to resolve the conflict).

You can use this formula to plan and rehearse your part in the discussion. Actually phrasing your concerns in this manner and asking to discuss the matter further is also a useful way to begin conversations about subjects that frequently lead to conflict.

10. To move toward a "win-win" outcome—one in which both of you get at least some of what you need, rather than fulfilling one person's agenda at the other's expense—make room for compromise. Before you actually discuss the matter, identify the best possible outcome (what you would get if you could have everything you want exactly the way you want it), your bottom line (the least you could accept and still meet your most pressing needs), the options that fall between the two extremes, and anything you are willing to give (or give up) in order to get your needs met. Not only will this provide bargaining chips to be used during actual negotiations, but it will also warm you to the *idea* of compromising. Instead of approaching the discussion expecting to "duke it out" until you get your own way, you are actually prepared to give a little so that both of you can get some of what you need.

When Should I Try to Change My Circumstances?

When you are not ready or willing to change yourself. Perhaps you could live with your government job if you developed more patience or accepted the fact that 50 percent of your time will be devoted to completing paperwork. Maybe you would commit yourself to your current relationship if you gave up the notion that somewhere out there the perfect man or woman is waiting for you. Or your in-laws might not get on your nerves if you forgave them for the less than complimentary things they said about you before you married their son or daughter. If you do not want to or are not ready to make those internal changes, but the situation is making you miserable, change the situation. Get a different job. End your relationship or separate temporarily so that you can date others. Spend less time with your in-laws.

When you have *changed, but the situation has not improved.* Maybe you don't let your boss push your buttons anymore, but he still tries to or is paying you back by giving you the worst assignments. Perhaps working the reception desk at a busy metropolitan hospital still drives you batty, even though you have done everything in your power to reduce your anxiety and be more organized. Or you may have changed your response to and even set limits on your friend's possessive behavior, but she still gives you the silent treatment or becomes nasty and sarcastic whenever you pay attention to other friends. If so, it is time to change your circumstances.

When you grow out of that situation. Because of changes in your attitude, behavior, and especially your self-image, you may find that you no longer fit the situations you have been in for quite some time. For instance, being demeaned or constantly criticized by your boss or your lover may have been tolerable when you did not think much of yourself and truly believed that the other person was trying to help you be a better person. However, once you gain more self-confidence and experience successes in other areas, you may realize there are better work situations and better relationships available to you and that you deserve to be in them. You have outgrown your circumstances, and it is in your best interest to change them.

When you can finally hear what other people have been telling you about your situation. While on auto-pilot, most of us suffer from selective deafness. Our friends, coworkers, relatives, and sometimes new acquaintances make observations about our intimate relationships, our work situations, or our over-loaded schedules, but we knowingly or unwittingly choose *not* to pay attention to what they say. Once we remove our blinders and begin operating with more conscious awareness, their words may come rushing back to us and we may discover that they were right—that we *were* being exploited at work, that we *are* taking out work frustrations on loved ones, and that we *were* taking on more than anyone could possibly handle. With our newfound insight and their support, we may choose to change those circumstances.

And of course, an excellent time to change your circumstances is any time *you want to try something new.*

How Can I Make Sure Hidden Agendas Do Not Keep Me from Benefiting from Psychotherapy?

To tell you the truth, no one ever asks me that question, but perhaps they should, since both the agenda you bring into therapy and your therapist's psychological agenda can have a dramatic impact on the therapeutic process.

The agenda you bring into therapy includes your motivation for seeking professional help. Was there a crisis—an unexpected turn of events that you are having difficulty coping with on your own? Are there issues and unfinished business from the past that are getting in your way today? Are you suffering from depression, panic attacks, obsessions and compulsions, or other emotional disorders that have not departed even though you tried to overcome them yourself? Have you encountered a seemingly insurmountable obstacle in an ongoing relationship? Or do you want to know more about yourself and what makes you tick? One reason for seeking professional help is no better or worse than another.

However, recognizing your motives enables you to be more specific about what you hope being in therapy will accomplish—which is another item on the agenda you bring into therapy.

Are you hoping to learn to make better decisions; manage stress; resolve relationship conflicts; become more assertive; rid yourself of a habit or addiction; be less anxious in social situations; cope with circumstances that cannot be changed; make a career change; or ensure that the next time you get involved in an intimate relationship it will turn out differently than your relationships have in the past? The more you know about where you want to go, the more likely you will be to get there.

But perhaps the most influential agenda item is what you expect from therapy and your therapist. You may expect a psychotherapist to have all the answers and give them to you; to make comments but let you draw your own conclusions; or to always accept and support anything you say or do, never confronting you in any way. You may be looking for a quick, easy fix. Or you may be terrified because you assume that therapy is a long, agonizing process. You may expect therapy sessions to stay focused on the problem you present or assume that you will spend hours on end discussing your early childhood and how your mother toilet-trained you. You may even walk into a therapist's office fully expecting psychotherapy to fail. The expectations and feelings you have toward any given therapist, based in large measure on what you bring in from your past, might loosely be called *transference*. If you bring your expectations out in the open and share them with your therapist early on, there will be fewer unpleasant surprises at a later date.

Some of your preconceived notions about psychotherapy may be entirely unrealistic, while some needs and expectations can be met by some therapists and not by others. That is why most therapists will ask you about your reasons for seeking professional help, what you hope to accomplish, and what you expect. If a therapist does not ask, you can (and will generally find it helpful to) volunteer this information. It is one way to determine if your needs are compatible with the therapeutic approach—and with the therapist's agenda.

Yes, we therapists, being human, have psychological agendas too. We have characteristic responses which are compatible with the theories we embrace and the professional training we received, but which may or may not be compatible with your needs and expectations. We also have old agendas, self-concepts, and expectations that motivated us to choose to become therapists and help determine the kind of therapy we provide. (Some of us are nurturers. Others are problem solvers. Some are intellectual model-makers.) Our personal motives create professional biases—as well as perspectives—which an effective, conscientious therapist recognizes and accounts for while working. Consciously guarding against tendencies to operate on auto-pilot, keeping our eyes peeled for things that our own biases might misinterpret or cause us to miss—including utilizing the characteristic response on behalf of you as a patient—are examples of working with the *countertransference*.

As a consumer who is purchasing the services that a therapist provides, and even more so as an adult attempting to make choices that are in your best interest, you owe it to yourself to find out about your therapist's agenda. At the outset, you can:

- express some of your doubts or fears and pay attention to the response you get;
- ask a friend or respected professional's opinion;
- review the therapist's credentials;
- ask about the therapist's experience, especially with treating problems like yours;
- ask how *this* therapy typically operates—what theoreti-

cal perspective is preferred, whether you can expect passivity or activity from the therapist, how long most patients remain in therapy, and what you can expect to go through during your therapy sessions;

· find out what the therapist's policy is on missed appointments.

Although you can gather some of this information over the telephone, I recommend at least one face-to-face meeting before deciding to get involved in treatment with a particular therapist. During that meeting, *what* the therapist tells you will help you determine whether or not your agendas are compatible. For instance, if you are seeking insight and personal growth and the therapist tells you that he or she uses a short-term problem-solving approach, you do not have the basis for a good match. Likewise, if you want help getting through a crisis and the therapist only does classic psychoanalysis, you may have come to the wrong therapist. Many therapists will tell you that they use an eclectic approach. Although you may think this means they do what is best for each individual patient, it may not. So, ask for more specifics. Also, and most importantly, pay attention to *how* your questions are answered and how you feel. If the therapist seems defensive or annoyed, dodges your questions, cannot answer them, or repeatedly replies by asking you a question, these are *not* promising signs.

Once you find a therapist who seems suited to you (and it may take more than one try), the two of you need to negotiate a psychological contract, bringing out into the open and coming to agreement on what you can reasonably expect from one another and your relationship. The contract might specify what you will work on together, how long you will work on that problem before evaluating your progress, whether you will be expected to do things like keep a journal, write down your dreams, or complete other "homework" assignments between sessions. Be aware that although setting forth these terms enables you both to begin your therapeutic relationship with your eyes wide open, it does not guarantee that problems will not arise at a later date.

Continue to monitor the relationship. Be on the lookout for the universal tendency to put therapists on a pedestal, to set us up as wise, perfect parents and then be disappointed or furious because we did not live up to the image you projected onto us. An astute and effective therapist will help you understand and work through your projections as well as guard against susceptibility to psychic inflation (getting a swelled head).

If you find yourself feeling uneasy:

- realize that some of your discomfort is a natural by-product of being in therapy. Old or frightening material may be rising to the surface and your ego may be trying to push it down again;
- do psychological spot checks to determine whether or not something you are remembering, telling yourself, or expecting to happen is the source of your anxiety or mistrust;
- use the hidden-agenda checklist to find out if you are receiving mixed messages from your therapist or responding to other signs of a hidden agenda in action.

Having conducted these reality tests, if you think your therapist may be contributing to your discomfort, by all means broach your concerns. A good therapist will take those concerns seriously and will *not* respond in a defensive, manipulative, or guilt-inducing manner.

Even if everything is proceeding smoothly, periodically review and renegotiate your psychological contract. As you change and grow, your needs and goals will too. Ideally, you and your therapist will work together to determine whether or not you have accomplished the goals you set out to accomplish and then mutually agree to terminate therapy or set new goals and continue treatment. In some instances, however, you will feel finished and your therapist will think there is more work to be done or vice versa. If your relationship is strong and healthy, you will be able to negotiate a compromise—for instance, coming to therapy once or twice a month instead of weekly or taking a break for one or two months and then meeting again to decide how to proceed.

Of course, you do not need your therapist's permission in order to terminate therapy. You can do that at any time and you can do it because you have gotten what you needed or because you are not getting what you want. Naturally, it will be in your best interest to be sure that you are making a conscious choice and *not* just fleeing because that is your characteristic response to demanding or unsettling situations.

When All Is Said and Done

For the duration of your stay on this planet you will encounter baffling situations. You will come across circumstances that bewilder and frustrate you, and people whose motives and modus operandi provoke, stymie, or hurt you. In fact, you will probably discover that, soon after getting past one trouble spot or getting a handle on one difficult situation, a new and different one appears on the horizon.

On the other hand, while no one can be guaranteed smooth sailing forever, there's a real thrill in knowing that you are now steering the ship. You know how to figure out what is going on below the surface in baffling situations. You have options for dealing with those situations effectively. You have the insight and information to make choices that are in your best interest. You have learned how to get yourself off auto-pilot. And as a result, you can plot a course around the eye of many a storm, and ride the inescapable storms with clearer thinking.

Then you will reap the ultimate rewards of the insight and conscious awareness you gained by reading this book— fully experiencing and thoroughly enjoying the days and nights of your life when the sea is calm, the sky is clear, and you are cruising along on the course *you* have chosen.

Glossary
of Strategic Maneuvers and Rigid Relationship Patterns

Strategic Maneuvers

Simple Secret Keeping: lies, half-truths, omissions, and cover-ups.

Deflection: Taking the heat off yourself by finding faults in others, criticizing the person who seems to be criticizing you or pointing out the flaws in their criticism.

Having a Problem That Isn't the Real Problem: Getting worked up about certain circumstances or scapegoating certain people so that you do not have to face your feelings or do anything about more threatening or unchangeable circumstances.

Creating Distance: Driving a wedge between yourself and others by changing subjects, making jokes, walking away, seducing them, and so on. This prevents them from invading your privacy or uncovering information that they might use to control or manipulate you.

Jumping the Gun: Deciding what is wrong and doing something to fix it without checking out your perceptions beforehand. This protects you from information that you do not want to hear or face—something that you fear the other person would tell you or blame you for if you gave them the chance.

Button Pushing: Exploiting people's vulnerabilities and sore spots in order to manipulate them into doing what you want them to do.

Softening Up for the Kill: Sympathizing with or flattering other people so that they will feel grateful, indebted, or close to you and fulfill a request when you make one.

Setups and Mixed Messages: Saying one thing when you mean another, asking loaded questions, fishing for compliments, giving people the silent treatment, and so on. You attempt to elicit the response you want without acknowledging that you want it, transmitting your message in secret code and expecting the other person to "get" it.

Creating an Impression: Playing a role, saying or doing things that lead other people to believe you are different (and usually better) than you actually perceive yourself to be. This masks your insecurities and presumably fatal flaws but also puts you on common ground with people whom you like and want to get to know better.

Nonacceptance: Consciously choosing not to "get" what is actually going on. Saying "I don't believe this is happening" when you do indeed know and believe it is happening but do not want to look at what it really means or what you might have to deal with because of it.

Distortion: Consciously altering the facts or explaining away certain unpleasant realities. You conjure up a reason for unpleasant occurrences and although you do not really "buy" your own explanation, it helps you postpone having to deal with the event.

Distraction: Knowingly taking your mind off your troubles by engaging in activities that focus your attention elsewhere.

Compensation: Overstating one side of the story in order to downplay the less appealing side, i.e., trying to forget that your in-laws are irritating and demanding by reminding yourself of their past acts of kindness and generosity, or whenever you are feeling overwhelmed or exhausted at work, telling yourself how exciting and challenging your job is.

Suppression: Temporarily and consciously pushing certain thoughts and feelings to the back of your mind until you have the time, energy, or resources to deal with them.

Rigid Relationship Patterns

"Don't Cross That Line or Else." Player one tries to increase closeness/intimacy. Player two pushes player one away. Player one retreats until she or he is too far away. Player two reels player one back in—until player one crosses the line again and restarts the cycle.

"Hide and Go Seek." Player one lets player two know that she is upset, but not what is upsetting her. Player two immediately begins looking for the problem she has hidden. Player one gives hints to let player two know if he is "hot" or "cold" and he keeps looking until he stumbles upon the source of player one's discontent or gets angry and the two players fight.

"Mother, May I?" Player one tries to get player two to do something. Player two overreacts in some way—usually by getting angry. Player one retreats and tries again.

"Village Idiot." Player one asks player two to do something. Player two agrees but "plays dumb" and asks player one so many questions that he decides to remove the responsibility from player two's shoulders and place it upon his own.

"Who's the Boss?" This pattern is similar to the previous one, only more extreme and more likely to end in an argument. Player one asks player two to do something. Player two agrees but "forgets," procrastinates, or bungles the task. Player one ends up doing or redoing the task and gets angry at player two. Thinking that she is unreasonable, player two gets angry as well.

"Yeah, but . . ." Player one has a problem. She tells player two about it and asks for his advice. He makes a suggestion. She responds by saying, "Yeah, but . . ." followed by the reason why that option won't work. Player two suggests something else. Player one counters with another "Yeah, but . . ." until player two runs out of suggestions. He is frustrated. She is vindicated—there really isn't anything she can do about her problem.

"You Decide." Player one asks player two for input into a decision that affects both of them. Player two replies, "I don't know," or "It doesn't make any difference to me," or "I trust your judgment," and tells player one to decide. Regardless of the decision that player one makes, player two complains about it. This makes player one angry, but also keeps the pattern going since player one, hoping to prevent player two's complaints, will feel compelled to ask for his input the next time a decision must be made.

"All Better." Player one says, "I'm upset," or "I feel yucky," or seems on the verge of doing something player two thinks he will regret. Player one is not hiding anything from player two and would elaborate on his feelings if she gave him a chance to. But player two immediately does or says something that she thinks will make player one feel "all better" or points out the misstep he is about to take. He resents this and they get into an argument or he is grateful for it because it absolves him of all responsibility for his problems (which she may resent since it puts her in the position of always mothering and rescuing him).

"Getting Even." In this pattern, both players have the same characteristic response, so it is impossible to say who makes the first move. One player does something that hurts, embarrasses, or offends the other, who gets even at the next available opportunity. The first person then evens the score, which naturally prompts the second to retaliate once more. The moves and countermoves continue until they have a "monster" argument that temporarily clears the air or one of them "calls a truce" by doing something nice for the other.

"Injustice Collecting." Instead of getting even at the first opportunity, player one, over an extended period of time, collects enough evidence against player two to justify "throwing a tantrum" or instigating an argument. Then the next time player two "messes up" in some relatively innocuous way, player one "freaks out," irately blasting player two for that transgression *and* all of the ones she had not commented on previously. Player two does not take this outburst seriously and goes right on doing what he has always done. And so does she.

"Dodge Ball." Player one "messes up" repeatedly and in retrospect realizes that he has been doing this and getting away with it for as long as he can hope to. Realizing that he soon will have to "pay the piper," as soon as he notices the slightest sign of irritation on player two's part (or simply feels guilty enough about his behavior), he does something to please or appease her. Player two forgets the transgressions and reminds herself that player one is sweet and considerate or convinces herself that player one knows that he "messed up" and is letting her know that he won't "mess up" again. But, of course, he does and then "dodges" her truly justified reaction once again.

Appendix
Unconscious Coping Mechanisms

The psyche uses the following unconscious coping mechanisms to conceal or camouflage:

- Your own impulses—the wishes, instincts, and urges which you are afraid could seriously harm you or others if you were to acknowledge or give in to them
- The possibility that you are not who you would like to be—not as capable, lovable, worthwhile, or in control as you believe you are supposed to be
- Your secrets themselves and the potential to uncover an incident from the past that you are afraid will devastate you and turn your life upside down

Like the strategic maneuvers you knowingly employ, unconscious coping mechanisms can be productive or unproductive, temporary stopgap measures or part of a massive, never-ending cover-up and either bring about positive change or make matters worse.

If your automatic agendas:

- lead to rigid behavior patterns
- are motivated more by past needs than by present or future realities
- distort your perception of yourself, other people, or your relationships
- eliminate the possibility of satisfying your needs (rather than postponing gratification when a specific situation calls for postponement)
- bottle up your feelings, preventing you from expressing emotions even when they're warranted and no real damage would ensue,

then chances are your coping mechanisms have become maladaptive. Instead of helping you cope, they are getting in your way.

If this is the case—and for most of us it is—you can take back the reins and steer your life in the direction you want it to go by gaining insight into your unconscious processes and their effect on your life. You must play Sherlock Holmes, looking for clues in your own and other people's behaviors. The following chart can help you identify the visible and audible results of using unconscious coping mechanisms.

REPRESSION (forgetting an entire event or the most vital elements of it)

You: Are tense, tight, and humorless in general or in certain situations, especially those calling for spontaneity, creativity, or the ability to "think on your feet."

Have irrational fears, phobias, or panic attacks.

Blow up or find yourself on the verge of tears under circumstances that seem minor or meaningless in retrospect.

Other People: Tell you to loosen up, relax, or that you look as if you are ready to explode.

Say, "Don't you remember?" and go on to describe an

incident that you do not remember at all or do not recall happening the way it is being described.

ISOLATION (acknowledging the facts but detaching and burying the feelings associated with a certain event)

You: Are numb, empty. Have a sense that your life is like a flat line, that there are no emotional peaks or valleys.

Perceive yourself as separate, different, disconnected from others; alone even in a crowd.

Say things like, "I can't remember the last time I cried," "I don't let people like that get to me," "I'm not going to let this upset me," or "There's no point in getting angry."

Occasionally experience rushes of anxiety, sadness, resentment, or other emotions that are not connected to any immediate circumstances.

Other People: Accuse you of lacking compassion or being cold, insensitive, heartless, or stoic.

Try to get you to talk about your feelings (to which you reply, "I'm feeling fine," or "There aren't any feelings to talk about," or "What good would that do?").

DENIAL (replacing facts and feelings about what is happening with your own version of reality)

You: Use certain catch phrases, including: "No problem," "I've got it under control," or "I don't know what you're talking about."

Tell yourself that people who see things differently from the way you do are jealous, judgmental, crazy, or troublemakers.

Other People: Seem to be making the same comments about you over and over again.

Ask, "Don't you see what you are doing?" "When are

you going to face facts?" or "What's it going to take for you to realize what you are doing to yourself?"

Threaten, beg, plead, or try to manipulate you into "seeing the light" or changing your behavior (to which you reply, "You're making mountains out of molehills," "I can't believe you would say/think that," "You're imagining things," "I am *not* . . ." "Who asked for your advice?" or just plain "Get off my back.")

⚹ **INTELLECTUALIZATION** (turning problems into interesting events and rationalizing your own and other people's actions)

You: Respond to an unsettling situation by immediately wondering *why*—why is he doing that? Why is this happening to me? Why am I feeling this way?

Explain your behavior after the fact.

Minimize your problems by comparing them to other people's, ones you have had in the past, or imaginary worst-case scenarios (i.e., "It's not so bad. Things could be worse. At least, I'm not . . .")

Use the words "Yeah, but" to open sentences explaining why you cannot change yourself or your situation.

Put other people in a position to explain themselves, asking numerous questions, including ones the other person has already answered several times over.

Say things like, "There must be a logical reason," "I'm sure there is some explanation for . . ." or "I will not accept that this is 'just the way it is.' "

Other People: Accuse you of badgering, interrogating or cross-examining them.

Become exasperated and say things like, "I already told you why I did it," "I don't know what you want me to say," "You're too defensive," or "Fine, don't do it. Just stop giving me these lame excuses for why you aren't doing it."

DISPLACEMENT (taking out your frustration on the wrong target or over an inconsequential issue)

You: Yell at or make nasty comments to sales clerks, cashiers, bank tellers, waiters, and other strangers, either feeling ashamed of yourself afterward or explaining away your behavior (They deserved it. They shouldn't have . . .)

Find that certain circumstances (Sunday drivers, slow checkout lines, waiting for elevators, the sound of your neighbor's stereo or your son's computer game) that are irritating in general become intolerable when you have had a "bad" day or are nervous about some upcoming event.

Create self-fulfilling prophecies, telling yourself that if a certain person does a certain thing, you will "lose it." Since this person is quite likely to do this thing—you get to "lose it."

Frequently encounter "the straw that broke the camel's back."

Refer to situations other than the one you are in during your outbursts (i.e., "I get enough grief from my mother, do I need it from you too?" or "I take orders all day long. I'm not going to let you push me around too.")

Other People: Seem tentative and wary in your presence, tiptoe around you, stay out of your way when you first get home or come out of your boss's office.

Accuse you of "taking things out" on them.

PROJECTION (seeing your own characteristics in other people)

You: Have "pet peeves"—find that certain quirks in other people's behavior irritate you no end.

Accuse others of being critical, intrusive, putting pressure on you, "making" you feel or behave in certain ways, backing you into a corner—often using the words "always" or "never" in your indictment.

See parallels between yourself and others, saying things like, "He's a chip off the old block," "We always see eye to eye," or "We're so alike, it's spooky."

Idealize certain people and situations, believe that you have found the perfect job or the perfect lover, but end up sighing, "He/she/it turned out to be just like all the rest."

Other People: Protest—"But I don't feel that way," "But I didn't say that," "But that isn't important to me."

Call you biased, prejudiced, or paranoid and may even say "You're projecting."

✦ INTROJECTION (placing others' characteristics into yourself)

You: Think: I guess I deserved that. How could I be so stupid, trusting, naive, etc. I should have seen this coming. I never . . . I always . . .

Have difficulty letting go; repeatedly review certain situations to figure out what *you* did wrong.

Decide that something would not have happened or everything would be okay *if only* you had or you could . . .

Feel guilty, ashamed, inadequate.

Try to "make things up" to people.

Other People: Say things like "But it wasn't your fault," "Stop beating yourself up," "Give yourself a break," or "Are you still worrying about *that?*"

ACTING OUT (*doing* something that prevents you from feeling anything)

You: Binge-eat, drink or use drugs, go on shopping sprees, gamble, have one-night stands, work around the clock, drive at high speeds—sometimes to self-destructive proportions and in spite of promising yourself that you would stop doing these things.

After the fact, think: I can't believe I did that. I shouldn't have, Why on earth did I . . . and feel ashamed, depressed, let down, or numb.

Tell yourself that everything will be better once you lose ten pounds, bring down the balances on your credit cards, catch up on your work, and so on.

Think over and over again about what you have done.

Other People: *See Denial*

PASSIVE-AGGRESSION (channeling your anger and resentment into being passive)

You: Are late a lot, forgetful, make sarcastic comments, bungle tasks, pout, sulk, accidentally misplace or damage objects belonging to others, don't hear certain things that are said to you.

Say things like "I was only joking," "Just kidding," "It doesn't make any difference to me. You decide," "I don't care. Do whatever you want," "Nothing's wrong," "It's okay. You go ahead. I'll be fine," or "Of course, it wouldn't be my first choice, but . . ."

Think: After all I did for them . . . Nobody cares what I think. Everybody's always dumping on me.

Other People: Accuse you of laying guilt trips, being punitive, driving them up a wall.

Get angry at you (and you wonder—but what did I do?).

REGRESSION (reverting to behavior you indulged in when you were younger)

You: Pitch fits, make faces or whisper and giggle behind people's backs, curl up in a ball on your bed or the sofa, stubbornly refuse to budge on certain issues, whine, look for sympathy.

Say things like "It's not fair," "But why can't I . . . ." "I don't care what you say, I'm going to . . ." or "You can't make me."

Get nervous, silly, argumentative, or act childish in the presence of authority.

Wonder why other people treat you like a child or don't take you seriously.

Other People: Say things like "Grow up already," "You're behaving like a child," "You can't go running home to Mommy every time something goes wrong," or "When are you going to stand on your own two feet?"

REACTION FORMATION (transforming your real needs and wishes into their opposites)

You: In any situation, consider first and sometimes only what you *should* do.

Are absolutely convinced that your point of view is the one and only acceptable perspective, especially on moral or ethical issues like pornography, abortion, sobriety, sex education.

Tend to suggest one all-purpose solution for your own or other people's problems—prayer, turning the other cheek, working harder, being nicer.

Feel guilty about feeling good, asking yourself how you can enjoy something when people are starving, homeless, fighting, sinning, and so on.

Other People: Tell you that you are being exploited or are "too good to be true."

Accuse you of being self-righteous, judgmental, or rigid.

Say things like "Don't you ever do anything just for the

fun of it?" or "There's no point in discussing this with you, since your mind's already made up."

Suggest that you are *always* "taking in strays, trying to save the unsavable, crusading, or taking on other people's responsibilities."

UNDOING (doing the opposite of what you want to or set out to do, trying to correct real or imagined mistakes)

You: Expect perfection and worry about making mistakes.

Envision disasters or predict negative consequences, thinking: If I say this, he will think that I am needy (pushy, dumb, immature, putting pressure on him, etc.). If I do this, he will reject me (fire me, laugh at me, feel hurt, go on a drinking binge, be depressed, etc.).

Plan to do something (ask for a raise, complain about the meal you've been served, speak up at a staff meeting, or ask for a date), obsessively think about it during the planning stage, but when the time comes to do what you planned, doing something else (ask about your boss's family, go to the rest room just as the waiter approaches your table, say nothing during the staff meeting, or line the shelves in your linen closet until it is too late to call for that date).

Go back to "fix things" or apologize for something you said, usually after "worrying yourself sick" about what you might have done wrong.

Check and recheck—some of which makes sense (like looking for typographical errors or making sure you have your keys) and some of which doesn't and becomes a ritual with a will of its own like checking for strangers hiding in your closet every time you walk into a room.

Other People: Say things like "I'm sick of hearing you talk about this. Just do it," "You're driving me nuts," "Let it rest already," or "For Pete's sake, everybody makes mistakes."

The coping mechanisms of anticipation, sublimation, altruism, and humor are fairly transparent and most of us can tell when we or others are using them. If you overuse them or use them when a different response would be more appropriate, they produce results similar to mechanisms that already appear on the chart—with anticipation leading to the same actions and reactions as undoing, sublimation looking like acting out, altruism resembling reaction formation, and humor taking on the characteristics of passive aggression.

Recommended Reading

Open and Hidden Agendas

Fisher, Roger and William Ury. *Getting to Yes*. New York: Penguin Books, 1983.

Goleman, Daniel. *Vital Lies, Simple Truths—The Psychology of Self-Deception*, New York: Simon and Schuster, 1985.

Kantor, Rosabeth Moss. *Men and Women of the Corporation*. New York: Basic Books, 1977.

Lerner, Harriet Goldhor. *The Dance of Intimacy*. New York: Harper & Row, 1989.

Automatic Agendas

Goffman, Erving. *The Presentation of Self in Everyday Life*. New York: Anchor Books, 1959.

Peck, M. Scott. *People of the Lie—The Hope for Healing Human Evil*. New York: Simon and Schuster, 1983.

Vaillant, George E. *Adaptation to Life—How the Best and the Brightest Come of Age.* Boston: Little, Brown and Co., 1977.

Old Agendas

Miller, Alice. *Drama of the Gifted Child—The Search for the True Self.* New York: Basic Books, 1981.

Miller, Jean Baker. *Toward a New Psychology of Women.* Boston: Beacon Press, 1986.

Psychological Contracts

Harvard Business Review Special Collection. *Managers as Leaders.* No. 90084. Boston: Harvard Business School Publishing Division, 1989.

Levinson, Harry. *The Exceptional Executive—A Psychological Conception.* New York: New American Library, 1968.

Self-Help/Change/Communication

Bower, Sharon Anthony and Gordon H. *Asserting Yourself—A Practical Guide for Positive Change.* Reading, Mass.: Addison-Wesley, 1979.

Elgin, Suzette Haden. *The Gentle Art of Verbal Self-Defense.* New York: Harper & Row, 1980; reprint, Dorset Press, 1985.

Freudenberger, Herbert J. and Gail North. *Situational Anxiety.* New York: Carroll and Graf, 1982.

Phelps, Stanley and Nancy Aushn. *The Assertive Woman.* San Luis Obispo, Calif.: Impact Publishers, 1975.

Simon, Sidney B. *Getting Unstuck—Breaking Through Your Barriers to Change.* New York: Warner Books, 1988.

Index

Jumping to conclusions *(cont.)*
   repetition of baffling situations,
      21–23
   stress, 14–16
   unsatisfying relationships, 19–21

Laing, R. D., 64
Lies, 31–32, 64
Listening, 230–231
Lose-lose approach to conflict
   resolution, 151

Manipulators, coping with
   awareness of exploitable points,
      209–212
   decoding mixed messages, 215–
      216
   neutralizing mixed messages,
      216–218
   reduction of exploitability, 212–
      214
Martyr complex, xvii
Mindset, positive, 183–185
Mixed messages
   decoding, 215–216
   neutralizing, 216–218
   as power play, 40–41
"Mother May I?" relationship
   pattern, 141
Motives, hidden, 9–10

Nonacceptance, 44–46
"Not Me," 93–94

Odd reactions, 78
Old agendas, 105–126
   example of, 105–110
   influence of family on, 120–125
   nature of, 110–111
   recall exercises, 111–119
Omissions, 31–32
Open agendas, 57–62
   benefits of using, 69–70
   checklist for recognition of, 59–
      62

defined, 56
disadvantages of using, 70
examples of, 57–59
hidden agendas disguised as,
   65–66
Oppressor, inner, 95
Overreaction, 48, 78, 100

Pain avoidance, *see* Self-protection
Paranoid shield, 65
Passive aggression, 212, 253
People pleasing, 209–210
Perfectionism, 211
Personal inventory for attitude
   change, 197–199
Physical relaxation, 191–193
Pleasure seeking, 26, 42–43
   See also Power plays
Positive mindset, 183–185
Powerlessness, 168
Power plays, 37–43
   automatic agendas and, 76
   button pushing, 37–39
   creating an impression, 41–42
   incentive for engaging in, 42–
      43
   mixed messages, 40–41
   set-ups, 40–41
   softening people up for the kill,
      39
Preconscious mind, 156–157,
   160–162
Premature conclusions, *see* Jumping
   to conclusions, consequences of
Projection, 170–171, 251–252
Promise making, 76
Protector, inner, 95–96
Psychological agendas, 53–80
   defined, 54
   function of, 54–55
   nature of, 55–56
   types of, *see* Automatic agendas;
      Hidden agendas; Open
      agendas
Psychological blind spots, xvi–xviii